T0290218

VICTOR QUESTEL

COLLECTED POEMS

ACKNOWLEDGEMENTS

The poems in this edition came from *Score: Poems by Victor D. Questel and Anson Gonzales*, published by the authors in Trinidad in 1972, printed by Rillopribt, Gasparillo; *Near Mourning Ground: Poems by Victor D. Questel* (Trinidad: The New Voices, 1979); and *Hard Stares* (Trinidad: The New Voices, 1982). Some poems had previously been published in *Pelican 69*, *Savacou 3/4*, *Manna*, *Now*, *Caribbean Rhythms*, *Caribbean Contact*, *Melanthika*, *Kairi*, *The New Voices*, *Tapia* and *Bim*.

Several poems appeared in both *Score* and *Near Mourning Ground*, but since there are no significant changes, they are printed in the sequence of their first appearance. For the record, the poems are "Pan Drama" (placed after "Seagull" in *Near Mourning Ground*), "Stage Directions" (after "Lament"), "The Epileptic Boy of February (after "Coconut"), "Down Beat (after "No Pain") and "Wreck" (after "Lines").

The poems are printed as they first appear. No changes have been made to Victor Questel's tendency to hyphenate whenever possible.

COLLECTED POEMS

VICTOR QUESTEL

WITH

GORDON ROHLEHR

"THESE COLLAPSING TIMES":

REMEMBERING Q

PEEPAL TREE

First published in Great Britain in 2016
Peepal Tree Press Ltd
17 King's Avenue
Leeds LS6 1QS
UK

© Marion Questel 2016
© Gordon Rohlehr "These Collapsing Times":
Remembering Q

All rights reserved
No part of this publication may be
reproduced or transmitted in any form
without permission

ISBN 13: 9781845232030

Supported by
ARTS COUNCIL
ENGLAND

CONTENTS

III
HARD STARES

Part I: Looking

PRELUDE

For Anson and Joe

PRELUDE

On receiving my indenture
I bit into the future
and chewed the past-

tajas of crematoriums
where
skulls sulk at the
extending bones
dancing the moon.

And here
a skeleton-frame of a
bill-board
hawks
the profundity of nothing.

And there
a man-
grove edging a shanty
quietly
exhales smoke the colour
of a glow-
worm.

Now
caught between the hollow knees of my existence
blinded by scan-
sions s-pewing
my alter-
ing moods
at the cross
roads of creation
I write,
doggedly, like a cur.

Cut by the rain drops
which fall with the
quick sharpness of
a child's laughter
chided into tears

grounded by the thunder
of frenzy turning inwards

trapped by the webbed
horizons weaved
by rainbows

I become a tiger and
stalk my stripes
of coloured solitude.

FRAGMENT OF A LETTER (ONE)

Daily I listen
to the bull-dozers
bull-dozing

into the hills

withering away

houses
hope and
truth

leaving us
un-
accommodated

and the
bull-dozers
never doze.

While you,
caught in the
glare
of the sea-
through
your shades
pulled tight
across your eyes

as a skirt
pulled tight
across an arse

I cite

blinded by
the shades
of things.

How the scythe
of that scene
cuts deep

though
one swallow of that
fleeting fact
cannot make

a somer-
sault

of this seasonal notion

FRAGMENT OF A LETTER (TWO)

Eating fig-
ments of time

wearing down the
dhotied birth of
notions which
haunts the
drum-head of
memory

I outsider
    outrider
    doubter,

feeling that tan
of pained complexion
cast on my face,

become my doubt
and from

this bull-ring of solitude
watch that pitching tour of your
protest harden to marble

gored to a public faith

BOYHOOD

legs akimbo
hands askew
she lay
buoyant
as water in cellophane

pained
pur-loining
a twisting
ScIN
tillating self
with a sneeze
of shock
at her fingers' tips

shocked
we squeeze
her fingers' tips
learning by our mis-
takes.

PAN DRAMA

Ex-
it
mas' man
push on
pan man,
a man
attuned, trapped

caught (like me)
making
subtle inden-
tations
in his
spider web

(now)
limbo-
ing from flambeau-
pan-yard
to
flying Pan Am

a-
massing cultural
missions

(then)
bombing down
the town
down

Frederick Street

to chipping feet
featly Jouvert
morning.

Wheeling across
the whole
cultural pan-
orama

now (like you)
armed only
with my
rubber-ended sticks

sick of your
blurred bourgeois
smile

pinging
           and
                   ponging
calypso tunes
of
chamber pot drama

or
racial melodrama

for colourless
mocking folk from
far away smog
lands
who

smiling or
like the dull

eyed miss
mincing dutch
sausage sandwiches
sighing

'mom they steal
the show

for
how attuned
they are
to their
base tenor
of
living'.

Trapped
attuned

making subtle
indentations
in my
spider web

I wheel away.

DOWN BEAT

A pocket
  myself an arse
a stick of grass
Pinching all to stay alive.
                   Head-lines   a sports page
                   Hem-lines   a body line
                   Glancing, heckling: all the
                                     time
                   Leaning on Ma Dolly fence
Waiting for time to pass
                   for the mark to buss
                   for the chance
                   to ask Chin for trus'.
                           Into Town
                   dark-glasses-glass-cases –
                   staring at faces
                   staring-listening-moving
                   Down-Town.
Welcoming Snake Eye
Out from gaol
with a fete,
                   sparing a hasty regret
                   for the ting
                   he rape
While remembering last night wake;
Working on meh sweet mas',
Clanging iron when Carnival in season,
                   For no reason
                   following some demon-
                                stration
Tuning in on the latest rake
or crash programme
Waiting for the next election.
                   Talking cricket-talk

Jiving on a side walk
Talking shit-talk
Like say
how many Left-Overs
between tea
lunch and tea
While with a forward defensive
assertive prod
stroking the 'beef' from the valley
Continually moving meh back-side
more squarer to the off side
near (a) gully
Dividing hours
into butt-ends, or romey
hands
or marking race
programmes.
Now an then
as Mighty Suck Eye,
serenading some tourists –
hustling some coins
for a
four-tirty
Lolling in a snackette
bush-rum quelling the pain
in meh guts
While the Redding
sitting on the dock.
Staring at the 'No Hands
Wanted' signs
The National Lottery Sold
here signs
and the long line ———
The lime near Marli Street.
Pulling at meh weed
Smoking out meh need

Cursing dem all
Forgetting it all
        Swaying down the kiss meh arse
        streets
        to a rhythm rehearsed in bed
        and the down beat in meh
                head
And overhead the sun strumming along,
lashing along meh back,
and I calling dat George
substituting half measures

for the w-hole.

SMALL-ISLAND TALK

Taxi climbing up. Lavantee like
is up Cotopaxi it going
and some people talking like
they never go stop a'tall

'Member Sky-High, Hands Up
Moral in the school yard,
Moralizing in the church yard,
Ole market on Charlotte St.

Manners for so   Is morning miss
Morning miss Lady   'member d'days
We wanted a goal and was
duck d'police or hole
the sinners or saints

Chile his Holiness consummation
in the Catedral while cricket
in de oval have some
pantin' in expectation

The Children's pageant spinning
across the grass
for independence
singing "now is a nation's
dawning…"

When every creed and race
could ah grass he cow
when and where he wanted
The nightsoil fellars or
sweepers passing in the night

Keats nightingale in Mr. Farmer
poultry class and we only no
'bout corbeaux flying over
de labasse

The kite-flying in the breeze
the morning washing under Mrs.
Maud stand pipe   the piping
hot water for the next
birth or bush bath

D'Doctor in the square
baby   Telma body in de
bag   look how Cinty gorn
to do nursing and cursing
Powell when she feels like
it   Dat is Democracy

Yer no Mrs. Maud
wasn't she mudder
look how he
lie 'pon she
large as life eh

Yes, dat is demockery
of it.
Today 'the river come down'.

LINKAGES

I

The donkey cart moves forward
with
the slowness of indentured peoples
with
the ease born of certainties
I
shall never feel

its rounded syllables
of movement
mocking
my liquid style.

The donkey
locks the
corner
and

you

dat son
of Columbus
steer clear
in your Datsun.

Who is the ass-
imilated man now

Kripalsingh
who sees
history in the landscape

can only pose
the question
can only pose

But how be judge
as well as
witness

who will advocate
the way
to windward

who will
sling the
last stone?

You,
you without
sin
poles apart from
the polemicist
anathema to
anansi?

How each blade of grass
cuts
the memory.

II

Our coming together
was as
absurd
as the twinning of cities

Her voice dumb

her every kiss
a diphthong of
doubt.

Such was the bought
fishy
sel-
fishness
of love
netted in a lover's throw.

III

Corbeaux
circle around
though there
is no carrion

only the oncoming rain.

The keskidee's
vision has
stuck in its throat

and still the inch
worm measures
the mari-
gold,
its length,
minds its own
interest
for profit or loss

IV

A frog leaps slowly
across the road
as my mind
leaps slowly across
the frog
as the road leaps

leaking fears as
my ruined gutter
spout
leaks.

I can no longer
avoid the
heresy
of hearsay
or
re-
dress
the naked
truth.

V

Vulnerable
as the
scarred mountain side

spare despair
thrown and
anchored
my dreams
I hang
on a nail
My fancy

since infancy
hammered
out.

Crying
I tear
myself away from
the scene.

The donkey cart stops
near
a museum

all art
becomes
artefact
now.

STAGE DIRECTIONS

A broken lamp;
a typewriter
      for sale
      or rent
A glass half empty.

Besides the girl
a tom-cat,
across the bed
a stray rack,
or two...

Photos of sunshine faces
the warmest things
in the room

Tom,
the cat, is just another
of those imitation things
to fill empty spaces.

Clips.
clippings
fragments of her
scattered like ashes
across her sea-
sonal sourjourns
in bed sitters.

She
handles
things.

Like a clock
her hands move
around marking
the hour

Like a clock
Her hour
never comes.

TOM

I

The wrong that are
our ancestors,
square the deal.

I have no grief
for words to
flounder upon

for the way lost
is the way
lost

and revolution
is the scandal
of poverty
sandalled to the
dust of processions.

II

Arches don't rise here
though for some
they fall with
each step.

III

To fashion consciousness
is
still to cut a figure,
yet another

pound of flesh,
have the gift
of the grab
steeled to
the mind.
It's anti-climax
my avuncular
smile said...

and here
triangular
betrayals
bay at the moon

necked to the crane of memory
yoked to the oil-
slick of our shores

waves of survival
for the slickest.

NELSON ISLAND BLUES

One eyed

grey
molotov monotony
swims around
reflecting the sky
bleeding ashes of
echoes out of my eye-
balls
breeding a foetus
future full of
scars left
(scar-
let ribbons of
voices cut)

and
silence
lies
sure

like the
fruitless search
for bullet-
ins
of the blown
bugle
whispered along dry grass

speared to my head.

SISTER

dizzy.
Who the Rass
am I?

she gently
goes mad
on my mind

her praying-mantis
attitude
has caught her

hooked her
to the blue eye
of Jesus.

'Reds',
yer pink-bullock's
eye
beams
the upcoming car-
riage to heaven,
to Jahhh.

My music
in-
sects me.

Bird,
      Beetles,
           Sparrow.

drunk.

The ship
limbos
my bar of sorrow

Dizzy, I'll
not play my strumpet
tonight

my girl is dead.

EBB TIDE

A cautious sailor steers
his craft economically
round a buoy

as his son
Tony, stares stonily
at the SURFace sun-
shine and

sees the tatooed arm
anchored in the tattered
ruins.

In the dark buoyancy
of sailing silence
things cancel themselves
out.

CREATION

The striptease
frenzy of
silent sweat
in houses

continues,
as I hear

the ticking
of minds set
to explode
like jawbones
jammed
squeezing the
triggered word
to pulp

as I hear
the noisy dream
of El Dorado
hatching in an ear

sense the rattle
of bones
Raleigh did not
pocket with his pride

while
somewhere the tree-of-life
leaves
us lax
like our
moral sense

somewhere
in the vacuum
of letters
lies
the nerve centre.

HIC JACET

As the Word
falls with ancient trees
the printer's devil
etches my faith
with the words 'Hic Jacket'.

This covers the isolated
fiction of commitment
which burns to its own truth,
as here
spare flesh points
a situation knotted

to the bone

rooted.

WHEN

Dis-
mantle
the cover up

Roll consonants
into constant
images

Wrap the Word
in a fist full
of vowels

Break
beyond the
boundary of words

Search your soul
for consolable memories —
sold out.

No post-natal, post-man
butterflies
after the dawn

'Cept the
scorpioned-creeping
suspicion
of failure.

How long the artist

How long the art

THE POET'S EYE

Another summer falls
that summa-
rises
our lies

as I
watered by liquid questions
sprout green fields
of despair
in this desert

see
the wet tar
reflect the
vacant look
of the highway's
crab sellers

eye
a nun
with her
man
i
fold problems
fold
her napkin
once more

as
stung tennis balls
screaming
from a racket's
cat gut
mourn her loss.

Flood lights.
weep for the Memorial
Park armistice
drowned in
history's shadow

as
a lover
sits silently
as the sad
half moon
over
the chapel's steeple
steeped in the ebb and flow
of her
love
shy in the
shade of remembrance.

God preys on my
mind
and spits it out
like a hawk
as i
getting down the streets
know the poetry of
survival
as a brother
glazes a well wrought
earn
from my
pocket

but who to sock it
to
now

as
scrubbed by the
datwan of anger
I, father,
dis-
pa-
rage
your truth.

MUSE

The bull-boy of skill
cracks

my skull

and your faith
gored
by the horns
of my dilemma

begins

our trial by silence.

THE EPILEPTIC BOY OF FEBRUARY

The Epileptic boy of February
in
sou
ciant to the price
of ruin

in
coherent
to history

like history is

passed
the
journey

the snail had passed
leaping from his shell

drunk on the rum
mage
that is language

hung up on a
rack and
ruined rear-view-mirrored
vision of reality

stomping his message
to a staccato
satchmo beat
more than he
realized

he was
a Krishna-Christ
in a sea
sonal light

lost
in a seasonless land
joining
the bearded bums

who bom
bard
the streets
singing
for their sanity

The Epileptic boy of February
felt the pain of nothing
numbing his mind

numbering his days

failing
to see
the ham
mocked
bamboo clump
mocking him

to the swing of time

Now
today
somewhere in the corner of
his skull
a tiredness grows

like the worm in your pea-green
heart

Today
tense with a terra-
cotta tension
he makes no
pre-
tense
fore
bears the tension
beneath the skin

Today
tossed on your sea-
island
cotton blues

making your
stations
shango-shocked
he grunts
the questions
Col-
trane asked

knowing now
that the
withering bamboo clump
was
preacher
mourner
the
deceased
buried in the wind

Today
and thrice on Sundays
a black Billy
Gra
ham
butts
his blues
to hell

Ex-
iled
now
on an
island
once
exiled
too early
to be
on that
de
so
late shore

reaping an
apprentice
ship
to loneliness

ex-
iled
once
on an
island
now
ex-
iled

somewhere in the corner of
his skull
your

tiredness grows

somewhere

WRECK

Jack of all spades, mastered by none
steered between ole mas' and half-mast
I cursed to my heart's contempt
needled by rhetoric, carded
for the threadmill, I follower
flounder

Sell
my frenzy to the Trade Winds
my beating
memory to the doldrums
and watch life's storm settle in
a tea-cup.

No politician,
I cannot
harbour hate
take your thorny existence
and bramble with your faith;
I will return to the cupped breast.

Hemmed in by silence
I skirt the pain
as this ruled life inches along
my palms
lined with the fronds'
reflection measured to
a tropical breeze,

Like a spider's seamy web.

My vision beached to a stare,
dogged
by the flea-bite of fear.

Hitting the bottle my faith splinters.

NEAR MOURNING GROUND

'Is like how education, wipe out everythin' San Cristobal got except the ceremony an' the bands. To teacher an' all who well-to-do it happen. Everythin' wipe out, leavin' only what they learn.'

    —George Lamming: *Season of Adventure*.

For

MOTHER
UNCLE SIMEON
GORDON and WINSTON

SEA BLAST

Those boys fishing by the *Federal Maple*
seem to be throwing their lines
for the lost idea rusting silently
alongside their meagre catch.

The islands' link is chained
roped
murmurs iron thoughts
sighs in pneumatic spasms.

The ship's captain will not abandon ship
he prefers this pause
to the dry-dock of his family life.

He's limp,
letters mean nothing to him now.
Can't spell his desires clearly.

Beneath him the ship lies secure
the tides do the work for him.
No manhood needed here.

She can take a cargo of failures
she took his well.
The captain is as drunk
as a fish.

Thrift for him is what is important
lying with her next to the pier,
the comfort of sea and land;
no need for a sextant here.

He is the lover sucked into
her pool's centre

her split centre of gravity.
He noses his way forward through
the wet vacant crab hole

as water eats into railings,
hurls debris against her
sides,
bird-shit paints the gun-wale
and
a port-hole gapes at the world.

She is a red crab holding on to a rock
hearing the sea belch her quarrels with
these islands she holds in her barnacled
hands

feeling the sea blast,
the sea's jawboned
wrath

as the boys leave,
but the captain hooked to the idea
is at the helm
charts a course he will sail no more,
never to come
to his senses.

SEAGULL

As voices lynched to a set summarise
a writer's winter aspirations
in this tropic heat

and an actor flies too close to the sun,
but fires one, bored as he looks at actors
burning to be the actor he has become,

but trapped in their roles;

you realise that they thread the flair
for the thing,

as everyone is arrested; as the flare
is bone hard,
bare,
horned as the bed

the island's centre, which is curved
according to your woman's crouch;

while you eat the knot that
has tied you to the ribbed tree reaching
for the sky,
mirroring the director's impulse of yourself
as you
listen to your knotted thought
circling
her rock of gibralta,
a stone's throw away from your palms
as you endure,
as the weather cock
your sole witness whirls with the wind stuck in his craw.

You are now
the stuffed fish on the mantle piece,
caught by the gull
like any actor
reflecting with one weather eye
that is not his,
or of his sea-
son.

LAMENT

There he stands. Reading a folded *Sunday*
Times beneath the street lamp
near Curepe Junction
a stone's throw from Soodoo's roti
shop

oblivious to the Baptist meeting at the corner
near Bata store. Neatly dressed, he wears leather
shoes, a black suit and tie. His eyes

shining a welcoming smile behind polished
glasses. Now a gentle nod of amusement takes
his head away briefly from the *Times*
as small boys mock his polished earnestness

and we speak. I've had my dinners you know.
I see. Marvellous place England, with her Inns
of court.

His accent fishes softly in the dark for a past
he knew darkly. Even the curl of the lip
in contempt at my asking him the time,
is soft

as he modulates that he only keeps British time.

Time could be mean; for that Grey's Inn
scholar's skull is soft,
on the fringe

as he stands folded on the brink of vision,
squinting ahead of our time,
waiting for the next Empire day celebrations,
even
as he holds a brief for these times.

VIEW

(for we two)

I remember the view from that gallery. The
sunrise she said

beautiful, the sunrise,

and I nervously spilled some beer on the rug
trying to take it all in. Paintings,
dogs, view and "Harry the Last". I looked at her
driving down the hill. We don't keep regular hours

my husband and I. So that's why the thieves never
bother us. Now you know the house come up

anytime. I never did. Now everything is at a loss

for the eye can't follow it all. The paintings, the view,
the dogs, "Harry". These last harried days.

She gently goes mad on my mind
hooked to the blue
caught in the tail-spin
of these collapsing times.

She floats
bobs and balances
breasts the tides
limbos again her bar
of sorrows

liquor fires her imagination;
that face turned towards me
is lit by the

experience of
books;

and looking at a boy flying a kite
on the hill,
mounting an extension of himself
and his
fantasy

I reel
rise and soar in the sky
then suddenly
feel the thread in his hand
go limp;
the kite ducks
drifts, ducks
and
      drifts through the smoke
towards the sea.

After the reel
we shared
dancing the earth's wheel
how can I speak with you again?

Santa Margarita pray for us
deliver us from our many accents and stresses
too acute for our minds.

THE WEATHER EYE
(for Leroy Clarke)

The sun is dying in the old way

slowly

as I turning with the recorder's spool
run
myself down
while longing for the stillness
of its centre

as the weather cock
whirls and the Bloody Mary
strangles my tongue

I am a stuffed fish on
tenter hooks
I am those lines and patterns
in that drawing
I am reeling
while keeping an open eye

for the new poet who
is an old painter
with his head turning to burning pumice
hoarding his talent with
a rodent's thrift
as he eats into the tribe's future
feeding his eyes

as he traces from fossil to foetus
the lines
beginning with Woman

endless fruit
through the valley of the howl
where the pain eats
each stroke

as he canvasses for the
memory of the folk
with a politician's blinding fury
using his everyword, everyword,
everyword
as a double axe
to split the myths that have fenced us in

whether you are snail or spider
keep
a weather eye open
for his track

FIRE AND ASH

i

The black cane trash soot is everywhere;
it is what reminds you that history
is still blowing in the wind
unburied
and unsung

burnt out
with each new season
that brings dust that
closes the Ti-marie's
eyes

even as WASA trucks want
'no riders'
as water strains against steel sides,
speed
and the sudden rise.

ii

The policeman's hands are windmills
grinding this morning's traffic
to a halt

the wheel of law within him
is wound up
perverts his brain
shrinks his baton
to a head

that can master elementary
rules
like 'Stop'

iii

For a moment he circles his mind's black-out.
He is now a frightened animal
caught in a headlamp's flame

he is the loose piece of flesh
that
paces the pavement

beating out its sole track
on the corner

the slack trade
that is trashing in its own heat
as he can't whip
up enough courage to ask for
a different beat

so like the ridden down trodden
mule he is
he kicks at history's stable door
and
turns his hands once more

grinding

COCONUT

Take a coconut
crash the eyes against a concrete floor
and watch the stale water run like
those sudden tears you wept
for the sudden time
of the triple vision of
maybe, perhaps,
possibly.

The sudden-time of the lost mind
in your head
that is cracked. Eat
the knot that has tied you to the ribbed tree.

Listen to your knotted thoughts ridden by each
vendor

but given balance by the steady donkey carts
riding home
late
through El Socorro

following only the whipped nose.

Now let your woman take a branch of a palm
picked
with her own hands
stripped by her broken nails

and make a broom that can sweep out the broken pieces
of shell.

Let this happen a stone's throw away
from everyone
so no one is clear about the broken pieces of skull
in that dazzling ray of sun
stroke.

NO PAIN

Tola trace is not like that derailed track
where
grass rides the abandoned carriages, still.

No. Tola trace is lines of rain
cold and hard like the hands that labour

or rain
blows in Ma's arse. Hole Pa back
he drunk bad

give Nanny the drum,
beat,
for Ma has gone
mad and into the forest,
moss growing from her palms.

The sky god is tall
lost in cloud,
the lightning can't flash him down
though it forks the trace

and lights up the many-eyed spider
as Balraj holds Panday's
hand
and walks the rice paddy

while Pa drinks spirits
and sees too
many

jumbies he can't control
so is blows

is bawling as, his son dies
without leaving a
trace in Tola's world

as the holy man farts during the wake's
rituals
'cause
maybe he is a
modderass chamar playing Brahmin,

a one-time hog
keeper
playing possum
playing de arse now like God.

What yer say
one-
foot,
as at the gate of cultures
Nanny raining blows
on the drum

and crossing water

WORDS AND GESTURES

I.

I can never quite imagine you behind glass
though that is where I think you are now.

Gestures ride the silence,

my cry
rivals the wood-slave's call
when couched between timber
and termites,

and the hurricane's eye
sees more than this near-sighted lover
of words

whose wanton absence of experience smacks of
a life-style
kissed away in solitude.

Smash your pane or
I'll burn out slowly between the lines,

empty as an unshaded sketch
shattered by the shot
blank
in your brain.

II

A snail in the garden creeps across,
losing my windowed stare in the undergrowth

and colour
runs along the darkening brain
dripping shapes to the glare of
half-blind eyes.
Possessed,
all I own
are my scribal impulses,

learning like any snail
that
home is where I'm locked in.

III.

But,
today is Carnival,
time's falling sickness
season
when
each shock of steel
mocks the strings of my guitar
and
masqueraders like their God
shuffle between the crib
and the cross
crabbing their stations to
prizes;
the ocean's roars of their life-blood
sucked into the sunken shells of drums

their life-style
caught in the glass eyes of cameras.

Lost in this folk-
mass

my cleft brain
paces Papa Bois's heel

feel my velvet gown,
my crown-
ing glory.

"Play mas' in yer mas' ".
I shuffle like the
rest
marred by my own make-
believe.

IV.

Daily
I feel the people's slow
strangulation.
My uncertainty
finds substance in shadows,
even the shadow of
life.

Though I write
doggedly like a cur
my insanity
out stares
my reflexion
and
even Nothing
now trapped
between skeletal bill-boards
has lost its profundity.

Look,

the search lurches tiredly
like my first
embarrassed
bongo
step.

V.

The iron mules in the oil fields
bray at my loss of balance
wink at
my slow grasp of words
green in their insanity
yellowing on the page

as I ride the rage
of your tide
each night of your harvest
moon,
rasping with laughter
as
the comic artist encircles me
in his lines

while
voices of mockery
creep beneath my skull.

VI.

Poised
like a painted
Adam
frozen between flight

and the sting of revenge,
the dual attitude of both
slave and citizen,

I
watch you make another conquest

as the country contemplates
itself
as a girl in her quiet hours.
I'll tell no one
for the whispered word now
could be the microphoned betrayal
then

VII.

The stickman's sojourn on the hill,
and
the snail's lonely journey
must both be mine; though walking
a straight line is not the same
as keeping your balance.

The soles of my feet
burn
your words
which attempt to trample
my endurance. Enter this gayelle
with me and I'll bois your ears
with language,
make your sex
drip syllables
into the sand.

So spit,
make your circle
and
square things off with your God.

The circle is complete,
the violence total.

It is the words
that are mad,
the words.

VIII.

And so
falling with every fruit
dropped by bats
my cry
rivals the wood-slave's call
when couched between timber
and termites

riddled
by its own gestures.

LINES
(for Robert Lee)

Frames cracked by Lines
of doubt
hold the cleft note that is blown
as you make that journey across this
blank
knowing that drawing the map is more important
than simply
journeying.

Stone. A slate that is wet
invokes a child's memory
of magic that vapours the mind;

Jumbie, jumbie;

perhaps
because it takes more than hope
to smash an image across these lines,
moving within like retreating rituals
erasing growing tiredness.

Articles of faith are not enough
as the hand that writes makes an arc,
a cave that you long to retreat to;

pure mist,
as you follow the tracks cut,
yet
tracing new lines. Watch at the scrawls
mounted like any bois-man's stick
following the craft of the hawk
and the call of the Jumbie

bird,
circling.   Your head is gathered in cloud.

It burns. It becomes the sun
and
only the raised finger to Arima
dares point at you now.

Shaping has risen in stature,
and again you ask,

how to be a Moko Jumbie without becoming stilted;
stone the blank with
stares as
tension rolls beneath the rocks of things
as you track the splitting image of struggle,
the next man's dream in print
but not what
you intended.

The slate is dry,
blank. Write.

The lines bridge
the cracks between the syllables,

the mist of collapse,
the need for height
as sprawled to a crab's crawl
you tread the eye's vision. Dream.

The blank turns to stone,
sounds fall again
from your swollen crutch of words
as the cave screams

as from the window of the bird's eye view
the bullock's hump looks
normal,
all things that are humped
level to their own
lines.

CLASH

Broken bottle
hurl
the razor sharp reality
of the clash.

Guts spill,
soil
Cito's small mas'.

is blows
is blade
is chop
is *Renegades*.

Pink Eye
waits at Green Corner,
cutlass cut
through the band –
Sailors Ashore

Vat 19 feet
stumble
down upon the blows
that explode:
All Stars

Police wave the flagman aside;
a S.P. marshals his
sections
for the Carnival

Goldteat smiles grey
does a dragon dance;

Devil's Wood Yard
bes' had
walk carefully.

NEAR MOURNING GROUND

Print tightened beneath candle grease like the drum-head
of memory
as uncle swirled suddenly to balance a point on
time
to the bell's appeal

as his eyes caught the staring shaking
brown robed whirl of my Spiritual Mother's
surrender
to Jordan
river.

She drew her shoulder blades together
rolled her lips,
noised a fit
and cut clean across the night air
of Curepe's oyster vendors,
coconut buyers
club-drinkers
and Maracas late-night travellers:

"Remember brethren to render
the tings that are Caesar's
to Caesar

and the tings that are God's…"

A child's hand slowly picked his nose
as he looked at the brass jar of leaves
and flowers planted on the
ground

as the Mother's eyes did not see apocalypse
though Shepherd, my uncle
had seen her private vision,
privately.

See uncle with red sash girdling his loins,
feet concrete hard scraping the cement
as he preached

the eyes tired but earnest
his truth riding as truth does
between poles of belief, the day's task
at shed five on the wharf still hard upon his back
though
soft-candle, aloes and water-
cress had done their best to make him
shed that pain

to preach about the Lord's.

Uncle delivered not a vision or a dream
but a text
mounted from the lost books of the Bible

calmly prepared the night before by the arc
of the kerosene lamp;
and the sisters beneath the street
lamp approved as Shepherd's crook
hooked
a few wayward souls

to the song,
"At the cross, at the cross where I first
saw the light…"

as uncle remembered the private vision
and the public pain,
the heat and fears
the stoning of the brethren.

Though flesh is weak,
persecution and the retreat to the bush
never choked their voices,

they had learnt that here
it was more important to confront
Jordan river than to cross it.

But Shepherd is like any writer
here,
a lonely pilgrim going to meet himself
a man burning on mourning ground

grounded by a vision of flight and travel
heat
and fears

weekend baptisms,
constantly trying to cross water
fasting
eyes covered by several colours of seeing
reduced,

returned and returning to the blank
page
trying to speak the vision clearly
though he cannot
without a text.

Listen uncle as the sisters hum us home,
what tract yer pull,

traveller,
mourner
man at the cross roads

after your years of aloes,
cutting through the creeping vines of age
hearing your parables of delivery
watching the bell-bottoms ringing out
a truth that leaves you sitting, tight
sensing only laughter, heat and fears?

Lord uncle say the word.

And uncle preaching since the time the Yankees leave the base.

FATHER

Father I remember your sweat seasoning
the dry earth

fertilizing the iron decks
you scraped with devotion
in the dead-
ly sun

swelling the seas
you have travelled.

Pacing water
chipping rust;

a boatswain to small island
sailors
without pride or purpose.

Now you hobble through simple tasks
that crack
your heart.

I can still smell your sweat in the air
from your weekend's returning,
armed with stories, jokes and complaints
about the men.

I can smell your distant letters buried
in the shit of mice, roaches

and
the stench of your decaying suitcases anchored
below the bed.

Today
I confess my love
for you

though we seldom exchange
more than nods

a quiet smile over the cricket score;

but we know
and
acknowledge each other's burden
sharing the occasional outburst of
anger
as communion.

Remember,
there was a day you
quarrelled with mother
and pulled at the clothes lines
and uprooted them
from the waists of trees;

now I circle
the fears
that
encircled you.

I too may uproot lines.

ii

Woman,
the knots in my hair are real

don't try to tell me
who I am
for
there are rages beneath my
skull
that only amnesia can
cool

so don't fool with powers you
think
you know.

See father, a man whose
feet are swollen like
his pride;

control over self almost gone;

that beautiful wreck is what
commitment can bring one to

love of home before self

so don't tell me about
faith,

one must draw the line somewhere
or else
grow old
and blind for causes that are not
one's own. See
that child marooned off
his own waters,
that is me, grown old and almost
harmless;
almost harmless.

iii

Father
you now lie rigid
with the final truth,
your posture telling me
things I only sense
as
the gap widens,
leads to places
unknown;
and I smell
our sweat seasoning
this earth.

GRANDAD

That shoemaker tapping
leather
believes in the little boy he is
talking to

has his faith tacked
firmly
in his sole
ability to survive

feels that the future
can be brought to heel,
controlled by one so young.

The shape of things to come
tightens on
his last…

The boy is six fingered
and borne the wrong
way
by decisions he did not make.

ii

No longer a boy,
he says goodbye to the empty
house

even as the hills exhale smoke.

There on the truck is
his old school grip
with his clothes, books
and testimonials

as he levels a look at
the road
and its beginning returns to
him

returns to the day he
first left
after gripping his mother

His things then included
a brunswick stove, a wooden plaque that
stared at him from the blank of its eyes
and a framed water colour
print.

Demons of flight fought
and won his sole
possession

his need to move beyond
himself

to ever-
last-
ing
heights

to claim a window in the world
as his

iii

The shoemaker's eyes
are blurred

he looks at the child in
front of him
darkening his shuttered
shop
and named him.

His thoughts criss-crossed
slanted
sank
beneath the child's skin

the child is still
the old man's search is
urgent
the situation is urgent

the face hardens to a glowing
mahogany

the sky screams
the horsemen
pursue him

he feels the suicidal im-
pulse
of his wrist

he jeers

taunts the hooves.

Still;

his thin voice is trapped in his
rib
cage
it is fixed as a dancer's
practised smile.

Now
a sigh pulls at the corners of his lips
evens
the triangle of himself

child
and child's future

as he tacks his hopes on him

DAWN
(for Marian)

Name this child
I peel my memory in
strips
and feel the old Adam in me
ease himself
out
of the temple   Rent
Renounce the world
the flesh
Just as I am
I come
Water washes against the shores
welcome
Christ is all   All is christ

Strip
immerse yourself in cloud
stained glass strains
the light
There the square of sky
               Green
green the markings on the altarpiece
I'm wearing the morning's calm
on my shoulder
du maurier's smoke hazes the vision
momentarily   The
schooner *Puntas Palmas* floats in the
water
I walk
palms point the journey
across the water

A frigate bird passes
even as
I sever all ties

nothing is in con
cord now
the zwilled mind startles on its own horizon
as
your child eases herself
                         out
and I name that light
Usha

ASH WEDNESDAY

i

Burnt out by liquor
I stumble words
that only the wind
hears
as you reach the end
of your endless journey
no end

as pink smoke rises
over the setting sun

and a discarded float

haunches with shame in a drain

its once proud dragon neck broken
like
that band's collapsed canopy
whose bassman is dead without
a shadow of a doubt.

But that's what this country is about,

the burning of flesh and cane;
the ash
of effort.

Find me that voice which
cried
"Land, Bread and Justice"

Find me that voice which
cried
"I come out to play"
and Today
I will show you

the splintered halves
of your twisted
self-
mockery.

ii

The music in my head
is still drunk
as I replace the seventh beer bottle
on the ringed floor,
the rings of water
trapping my down-ward stare.

Remember,
the game is blindman's bluff;
but the end
is when you pin the tail on yourself.

iii

Put on the light,
there are too many sounds
here
I cannot name.

No eyes like Heartman's
patient heroes,

I burn silently in my den,
seeing
each shaven convict's head
reflect a blind future,

Pacing the room
I go north from the Demerara window
only to be drowned in the paper
gulf
pinned on the wall

as my hands grope between
the Dragon's tooth
and
the Serpent's pointed grin.

It's all mapped out.

iv

Already,
that raised hand
that flings your garbage,
balances the ash
on your child's forehead,

stalks his future dreams.

Look,
a staring finger paces the sun's dead centre.

COUVADE

(for Wilson Harris)

I'm a sleeper of a tired tribe
staring with a fish's eye
seeing the circle we draw
while pursued by quick eyes of night

here where there are always the caves
the need to avoid the net of stars,
the urge to capture the awakening
touch of feather or scale

threading through the embracing rainbow.

Now eyes hunt the dream of history
cross the bridge of tribes
trace on walls of memory
the war-paint's final riddle

coughed by a lizard –
Where is the Nothing of which the sages

spoke.

VOICES

*(A selection of oral poems dedicated to Edward Brathwaite,
Anson Gonzalez and Cliff Sealy)*

I: THIS ISLAND MOPSY

'No Slip a deep Gulley
Ah man in leg trap believe me
Ah clean bowl every woman back to the Stand
Because they couldn't read the flight
Of me China Man.'
The Mighty Bomber.

Listen to this story
'bout meh long time Mopsy
Listen to this rumour
'bout meh girlfriend Sandra

Now this was a real happening
come home late one evening
find Sandra groaning
de girl
She didn't want meh loving

Chorus: Woman come in different shapes
             different sizes
             Offering different poses
             different prizes (Repeat)
             I might look like Mickey Mouse
             but I always have woman inside meh house

Look at meh crosses Lord
meh Mopsy calling the Mighty Crucifix ah fraud
Look at meh crisis Lord
meh Mopsy claiming I was a fraud

Come home no food in de place
She hair undo

tears all over she face

Ah get blasted vex
pull out meh bull boy
and bus' it across she chest

She fall down on she knee
and cry as hard as she can
stay please
you is my man
you ain't fraid to mek meh bawl
in pain
from right now ah go start
loving yer again.

Boy yer see dis creature call 'oman
don't bother wid no gentle touch
rough she up don't mek no fuss

Treat she like how the Multi-national
treat dis territory
sink yer hand in she country
what yer get take it for free

Extract what yer coud before she start
to fret and boil
When she sugar done
man drill for oil
Then break all ties
ignore she consternation
and leave she wid a new
growing population.

Chorus: Woman come in different shapes
             different sizes
             Offering different poses
             different prizes (Repeat)
             I might look like Mickey Mouse
             but I always have woman inside my house

II: SHAKA'S CYCLE

i A Light

Brothers and sisters raise the flags
wave the flags of victory. Let the enemy
see red.

Today I looked at mama and said,
mama, today your son will lead his people
out of this morass

and mama said go son,
do what you have to do, but
to thy own self be true.

So here I am this afternoon,
and already we wave the
flags of victory.

Let them know that we are armed
we have arms
we have access to arms.

Let them know that the people are
on the move
let them know that
we are on the stage of history
and shall not be moved.

Let them know that this is our
moment of revenge
when we all have
to do whatever each man in his heart
thinks most right to be done
about the *atrocities*,
that befell our ancestors in the past.

I am thinking brothers and sisters
of all those souls that are lost in
the sea,
lost, cannot return home

cannot ever find land
lost in the Atlantic
lost because of the Slave Trade –
a white man invention.

And dat man,
dat man,
(it is definitely impossible to help dat man now)
we must haul his tail from Whitehall
dat man is responsible for all that we see here today.

We have to deal with that betrayal. We
will deal with it when we make our choice,
and
Shaka say the choice is Liberty
or the Cemetery.

Support is growing
the marches are getting bigger
and we all know in our own hearts
what we are going to do.
I say no more. No.

When Black people move we
move as one. You know that,
so there is no need for me to say more.
We know where the guns are.

We know what to do when
the moment comes

as they say, we have to
seize the time,
and time is as tight
as a clenched fist.

ii Burning

So here we are
here we all are.

They say it could never have happened
it could not happen
here
it has happened today.

Remember how the heat lashed our foreheads
cracked our skulls
how the hot pitch bruised our heels
how our hands cut cane. The march goes on.

We know what we will do. We
know where the guns are. When the time is right
we know what to do. The Black man has always
known what to do. Let the drums roll.

So much to be done.
Shaka seldom sleeps. Let the hands, of Lakshmi
wave the flags.

iii The Final Flame

The question I suppose you are asking
yourselves is where we went wrong. The
question I suppose you are asking yourselves

105

is how they catch Shaka. The question
I suppose you are asking yourselves is
what we do now.

The fight goes on.

Some of the brothers have taken the fight
into the hills. They have taken the matter
into their own hands
and into the hills… Each

in our own heart knows what to do.
You ask me to speak about
my feelings,
about my experiences in prison.

I feel too deeply about these
things
to speak of them now. I feel
too deeply.

We need more black sounds.
Black people know what to do. We
have always known what to do. Shaka
say is the fire next time.

III: SCARECROW

(for Rawle Gibbons)

i

He has been horse and river,
has been ridden, bridged
and dammed;
better drummers than you have
tried to keep him out of
their inner circle,
but he is their master
for he seeks nothing.

He has been river and horse,
has been dammed, bridged and ridden
into dust,
better drummers than you have
tried to keep him out of
your reach,
but he is your master,
and seeks nothing.

You turned him into sticks,
flayed him with used
cloth, and made him scare
birds, beasts and
man.
You said you mounted him.

Now, he is hoarse
no lavwe
burns his lips
and
with water and ashes you
cast him out

bar your gate to his step
raise your sword
and banish him with one stroke.

ii

Silently he built his tent
his temple
and taught his daughters the strength
of his embrace;
the anteroom built,
the journey to his five
strong points made. He learnt to hammer
words to star dust,
and to whip the streets with
his spirit lash,
his bull-pistle of belief.

And then politics discovered him and his flock,
he granted the leader
power and they were granted acceptance.
Then, that man came,
and he took him
and showed him the five strong points of
this land
and put him twice on mourning ground
and told him his number was four,
and the door was opened
unto him.
Today, that is the prime millstone
that Shepherd carries now.

iii

We should light every candle
on each branched candle bush tree,
chew on carili
bathe with zebba pick,
paste on wonder of the world
with soft candle
and stain every finger of every breadfruit
leaf red, to heal
our political sin.

iv

But you saw it all.
You who can recall the smell of
infantol
soup and
the dust of school benches;
never benched, but always broken
and too well spoken for your
class.

Heard,
the humble decision to make dat boy
into a somebody,
but you never shared that dream; remained
a nobody with no dream
a drifter who saw the lack of
meaning too early for his own good
making message
and buying goods
with lightning speed

lost only in wonder at the starched
grandeur of his grandmother's
Bibled dignity wrapped in yellow, blue and
brown,
a Bajan who loved the Palm Sunday march, a good sermon
and clean salt butter.

How could God look down on one of
his own and watch her
lose her mind
and plead with neighbours from the past
for months before going
over yonder,
still baffles him.

Years ago her hymns would bless the house each
morning;
her room chalked with cabalistic markings
he never understood;
voice and vision gorn. Rest. Leave the rest to him.

v

He is still lost.
Never really recovered from
sitting through long hours
of lonely toil with
figures
cramming for an exam he will never
pass, preparing for a style
of failure he will later pass by.

Finally,
an act of trust was
rewarded with a violence
of language

that is still burning
within his skull,
kept alive by its own organic growth,
separate from his will.

This handicap he is running is his
last,
he expects abuse behind each eye-lid,
each kiss,
each handshake.

Abuse is so close to the listerined breath,
he lives in his darkness
alone,
more separate than
any stone

more hardened than any whore,
a man cut by family and commitment
a man that has become the vice, the tic
in your own head.

Yes, he saw it all.
There is no gratitude there. No
imagination. Nothing to capture,
but nothing. He
saw that blank early and fled.

Things still seem strange,
and pointless,
explanations too simple;
but at these cross roads
he will speak. Ashes,
water and tempered steel
can't seal his fate.
There is a meeting here tonight.

IV: THE MEETING POINT

Tonight,
you might find that
you face,
the sudden and final flight
into E-
ternity
no turning back
from
the fast falling of the evening tide.

Tonight,
you might find
your tongues aflame
with private truths.

Tonight you will feel
POWER
the ever working Power
found in the blood
of the Lamb,
Amen.

So, Sisters in Christ,
let the candle grease of
faith
burn to the depths
of your hearts

earn your place in Christ Kingdom.

Let us not leave here
a broken heart,
a fount of tears…

For only God is the answer
only
he
is your maker

not the politician weeping
into the wayside –
wayward microphone
not
the stone studded
statue gazing into
the wilderness of your
bewilderment.

Ooho
Brothers from CROSS FIRE
only God
is your sponsor,
only he is Life's
arranger.

Brothers,
don't let
your feelings be
trapped in a groove
of steel

Noah's ark
must remain
your canopy of sound

the flight of the tenors
your dove
of peace.

Children of Zion beware.

Beware of the blue bottle
in Time's garden.

Beware
the beetle's battle with
the praying
mantis

Beware of the spirit-lash of fate —
Nature's drunkenness.

Beware of the maljo of diseases,
Jehova's witnesses
hovering like flies in
dry season.

Children of Zion
don't be squatters
in the valley of disbelief

Children of Zion
you won't be squatters
in God's heaven

Children of Zion,
only believe.
ONLY BELIEVE
Amen...

Bang/bang/bang/bang/bang
bang/bang/bang
bang/bang/bang/bang/bang
bang/aannnggg.
Bang/bang/bang/bang/bang
bang/bang/bang/bang/bang/bang
bang/bang/bang/bang/bang bang/aannnggg.

O Gord our help in ages pass
our hope for years to
come.
Our shelter from the stormy blast
and
our eternal home.

Evil spirits are now cast out
from the mouth of this chapel,
this road-side tabernacle,
this sacred ground
these four corners and
the bounding centre.

I come with a message,
a message for all you lost souls
you children of Ham,
you lost high-strung
ham-strung generation.

This message I did receive in a dream.
I saw a well,
a pond, a pool
of water.

and this water was slowly
turning red.

We must turn to God,
repent and
be baptised. There is no other way.
Repent. Then he, the Almighty,
will show us the way out of this
wilderness. A new Moses will stretch
forth his rod.

Badang/bang/bang
badang/Bang.
Badang/bang
Badang-bang/badang/bang-bang/badang-bang.

Hear the word of God
when he does cry
does cry
does cry

No sinners will be left
in the rain
no stone left unturned
to save your soul

God is a good God,
a blessed God
a blessed God
a blessed God

A true saviour
the maker of heaven and
earth
heaven and earth
heaven and earth.

The wandering boy
will be brought home
tonight
he will sleep in the arms
of Jesus
of Jesus.

The mountains shall be brought low
the lamb shall lie down with the lion;
heaven

and earth shall pass
away
but my word shall not pass away
saith the Lord.

Badang/bang/Badang/bang
bang
Badang/bang
Badang/bang/Badang/bang
Badang/bang
Badang/bang
Bang/Bang
Bang/Bang
Badang/bang aannngg.

Let not the cock crow thrice here
tonight

No tear of Hell's fire here
No fear of the serpent's crawl
No fear of God's call
No prayer of forgiveness will
go unheard
Unheard.

Give thanks. Badang.
Break bread. Badang.

Burn in his holy word.

Let the bells ring out his truth
clearly...

Badang/bang/Badang/bang
bang...

V: GOOD FRIDAY

Bang/bang/bang

Bang!
They are shooting
They are shooting now
They are shooting now like stars.

Drunken tin-star sheriffs
lost star boys
in a film of our making.

The scarecrow has
risen
and it is blows;

John de Baptist dead.

They beat him in John John,
his deposit of faith
lost.
He broken and beaten.

They don't shoot shit
no more;
de man dead.
His teeth broken combs
His breadfruit head bus'
His phallus ripped
but dangling its length to his knees

His buttocks hung by rope,
and the crows are laughing
the crows laughing.

They hung each man
from a lamp-post,
a cynical light.
placed on their head.

Here,
every tree reflected their destiny;
men who opened their arms
at the cross-roads
promising a New World
of mud, love, cow-shit and
holy communion,
were shot and beaten.

They drop their blood softly
at the entrance of
every gap
and track
in this land.

The bell's tongue can't
silence those spirits
that are shooting
more deadly than big John Wayne.

Woman,
cut down their bodies,
wrap them in coarse
cloth
and bury them with your hate;
soon it will be Easter,
the glorious morning

when Tom, Chin, Harry
and Harrilal,
Mary,

Mai
Rosita and Clementine
must bear witness.

They beat him in John John
and the crows,
dey laughing.
Christ, dey laughing.

VI: MAN DEAD

(A poem to be performed with drums and voices.
Dedicated to Errol 'Stork' St. Hill, Andre Tanker and Michael Coryat)

Mooma,
Mooma...

Man dead today
spit
cross my path
and
that's yuh last journey,
Damballa will damn de man who touches me.
Chansay
make yuh play
reach if yuh reaching.

Mooma, mooma
yuh son in de jail
arready
yuh son in de jail
arready
take a towel and
ban' yuh belly.

Gall is my rum
violence my chaser
violence my chaser.
Gall is my rum
violence my chaser
violence my chaser.

I was the goat
which spawned the first drum

I am that man
who killed Cain
given half a chance
I'll kill you again.

I
son of Shakespeare
tutor of Webster
guide to Shaka
sponsor of Coffy
Daaga's real fadder
Satan's only horn child
by his sister

I man who
coach
Morne
Diablo's
Massa
Hood,
P.
Town's Tan
Moses,
now
damn you.

If ah die, ah die,
If ah die ah die
in mih country

if ah die ah die
in mih country
take a towel and
ban' yuh belly.

No bois man no *fraid* no
demon
no bois man
no fraid

No bois man no *fraid* no
demon
no bois man
no fraid.

I time's accomplice,
the insulted princely
toad
who squats on injury

I
who have killed every spider in the crack
now
crack open your spider-soft
skull.

Tajas of crematoriums
are all you will ever dance now.

Not even the sulphurous stars will light
your way
the moon will be drunk
with revenge. The sun
dark
with glee.
The horsemen shall ride
again
and
on your grave
the sky will refuse to rain.

Yuh in de jail arready
Yuh in de jail ar...rea...dy.
Take a towel and
ban' yuh belly

Mooma, mooma
yuh son in de grave
arready
yuh son in de grave
arready
take a towel and
ban' yuh belly.

I who gave God
knowledge of Hell
I who can sweat my
ancestors' pain
at will
now watch douens walk
nine times
over your grave,
and hear

Mooma, mooma
yuh son dead
in de country,
dat man
dead arready
No towel,
can ban' dat
belly.

Mooma Mooma
mooma mooma...

TRIANGLES OF SOUND
(for Soo' and the Q.R.C. Jazz Club)

Zanda pounds keys
conquers worlds
in his head
as
he balances on piano-
stool

neck moving like a bird's

as he yokes
experiences.

He is above the music
above the scent of all things
as
they play 'Saltfish'
and
'Sweet Breadfruit'.

Lost on the bass

pride swells like
the leaves
of a scrap book;

here they pull strings too

the guitar's neck
points
nods of approval

fingers stroke a beard
teeth smile

Lines take up the slack
between poles of
time,

of trees
and versions of green.

Flat.

Shift the key;
minor
few cords
the theme
then expands

expands
like his eyes

dew falls
on his eye
lids

covers
the present.

They are coming,
the eye balls turn
with the spin of
the drummer's wrist

hear it turn upon itself
it breaks out

wider

hands explode,

calypso is no longer repetition
trapped between tempo
and
the roofs of tents.

Rim shots send us
on the edge,
we balance;

the knots in my hair tighten
become taut
across the bridge
of sound

kinetic
sheer electricity

the scalp
is alive between
your ear drums

your feet float
across the water
of sound;

look at the bass man
rooted to the
tree
trunks beneath

his feet;

the boards sprout
my feet,
shake off the effort of plane
and chisel

and return to roots
water,

the Black Line is
shocked out of its
harbour

the bow is pointed,
    augmented
it narrows your gulf

they shake the scales off our eyes

amnesia no longer
drops from the fork
of the hanging tree

for we are
tuned in
turned on to a totality
that defies
formula.

The sounds cut
and scrape the memory

the bass bludgeoned
stilted
attitudes

the wire brushes
rip the skins
till
knowledge prickles our hair.

The triangle
of piano
drums and
bass

tightens;
the flute, an arrow
now
stretches that bow
of vision

the fingers of
the breadfruit leaves
point us home
as
I bleed milk that
hardens
and tries to trap the bird

but those cats
are in our garbage
and that sweet music
is where
it's at –

'Sweet Breatfruit'
and
'Saltfish'.

The rubbish heap
is a bird-lime
that none here
can escape

see the piano man humped
on top of the music

is blows
is blade
is chop

The triangle around the neck
loosens

the journey across
the three points
becomes
both pointless
and pointed
now.

The other woman
is both a nuisance
and a
balance
a wheel
a weight

feel the circle she turns
on your axis
look how she angles.

The bass man is asleep
piano man
is lost in flight
the high hat
fits tight

the bridges are
burnt.

The triangle is
a trap,

a hole in the sky
in the ocean

it swallows
iron birds
freighters
liners
pirogues
just so…

everything

becomes an
ant-hole
a crab hole
a pond
that breeds
mud fish;

the stench,
the rage is red,
symbolic
a blood clot
a blood clart
that absorbs
all things that are red.

"Reds
yer pimp,
yer pimple face
son of a bitch
yer still
riding shot gun
wid dem boys

dem does
read music yer know
dey does swallow
quavers and grace notes
with a rare, primeval ease!"

Freeze.

Ruins,
broken blocks
dead lumber

Miles
or lines away from the triangle
in P. Town
the old mission site

the original foundation
of a city

the rift of history lost,
only the triangle looks one-
eyed
at the ruins we cannot find.

though
even now
'Saltfish' is taking us there
to all the old ruins
the deserted cities
and villages of this land.

Keep
the skeleton of the tune
then expand.

Look there are the ruins of
the village of Cascade

whitened out of the map,

de Blanca where
hunter
and dog
skin 'guti
while the houses on the hills
look down on the
ruins.

Shift the key;
no cords tie
you now,
you are floating down

you have suddenly been
zwilled
broken bottle
and dog-
shit
have cut you through;

the music has high-
yoed you.

"Hi-yo
hi-yo"

The triangle tightens
the head lolls
all things
loll
roll
bob and bounce…

your skin is still
as tight as
the drum-head,
smooth as
the rubber plant

decorating the bank;

you spin
keep time
with the musician's heel

you wheel

water

see, three eyes
of a coconut judge
you;
everything is tight like these times
everything is on loan once more.

Keyed up
high strung
am as tall as Tatil
and better structured.

Struck by
all this
I turn,
the musicians are gone

the amp is
hung by its
own cord
velvet strokes the flute

the bass
doubles in
laughter at my lost hands,
the high hat is
hung
upon a peg I can't reach now

the musicians are gone.

I have sweated out
a whole experience

I am returning to stone

lost days
still
encircle me
cases are closed

the piano's eye-lid
is shut
the gayap is finished
I have returned from the triangle

I sweat last night's alcohol
unto the page

I edge my way
forward,

still on edge,
but with a greater sense of
balance
for I heard musicians
drenched in the water of their own
belief

place notes between and
through the lines
of my thoughts

through the mud,
the slime
the gut of all things

our history and our hope

sucking on the saltfish bone
of endurance

realizing our wildest
dreams.

VICTIM

'*Woman hold her head and cry*
cause her son had been
shot down in the street
and died
Just because of the system.'
                    Bob Marley, *Johnny Was*

The victim
waits;
he is fired in his tracks
fixed
stopped
stretched out;
the bush grows into his wounds.

He is riddled with a truth
that all will share. Once, he
crawled on his belly
now
slowly he becomes tired of the crab
antics that scratch the surface
of his skin
plunge him into a rash of
indecision
imprecision.

The family line is broken
again,
fractured like his skull. He
longs for water,
the bay leaf baths,
his mother scrubbing him.

He is at the stand-pipe
blue soap and
practised fingers
cleanse him. Now
he lies in the
bed of a river
with his throat cut
his energy leaving him.

He is floating in his
flaming silence,
a shot has fired him.

The mother looks at her son
and the eye bleeds;
she stoops and wipes
the jumbie beads of
sweat
whips the running ants
and waits.

The guerillas
wait
Kojak waits
for the cameras' flashing
flame of
approval.

The corbeaux wait
but not for the rain,
as
the eye bleeds
water
as from a broken branch
while the bullets rip, nail,
leave wales

welts,
hammer the home-grown truth
mock the imported disaster
that grabs the
head-lines
the eyes of the statistical bureau
while
the dead leaves in the
garden go unmourned,
the vines' murder of the trees,
the garden slugs strangled by
Aldrin
do not make *The Bomb*;

the stoned lizard
does not capture the reporter's
vigorous search
for the news,
the blight engulfing the hibiscus
will not make tonight's TV
panorama
as the hills mourn
the ghost of their existence
in smoke.

Now his back hardens,
he claws the air
and
sightless eyes watch
his tide return.

A door slams;
wheels
turn.

Her eye breeds
water;
faith;
takes root

takes years.

Blood.

CORNER STONE

The sleepers lie soundly here. Smell the
sharp raw wood that cuts the air,
the carpenter's finger

drops blood into the earth
building on ritual as the busted thumb
nails his savings into the effort.

The boxing is removed.

Look, the red poinsettia waves
the triumph of the raised roof. It houses
everything. Lines are run,
bring power to the louvred vision
as all the finishing touches are
tied off at the junction-box end. The fence
is up. We will live together here;
behind drawn curtains, stoned by work.

HARD STARES

For
Marian
Sonia
Nikita

PART I

LOOKING

Look at you
Truer than the body you inhabit
Fixed in the centre of my mind

You were born to live on an island
— Octavio Paz

THE BUSH

You are in the bush;
the thicket of things. Frogs
spread the word and

mosquitoes bite whenever they can.
Now,
away from the harsh glare of rock,
the sting of green
burns the eye.

You can't masquerade in the bush;
it has its own rules. Strip to
the waist and wade through
a tangle of vines.

Men have been doing this since
the beginning of time – clearing
their minds of the bush
by entering its pain –

hacking backwards to the first tree or thorn.

Quietly the bush swallows the cut path.

DIRT

Cracked boulders
pebbled stones
rubble of dust
grains, specks and flints of colour;

You possess something here. A fleck
of conscience; something to be
committed to. A reality

that moves beyond
deposit slip,
insurance policy,
cheque book,

letters of introduction
that sell the cash flow of stability.

Your head is balanced better than their books.
It reels with the red dirt
that comes down with the
rains...

Settles as silt,
then hardens your vision.
These runnels of your colour
are all that matter.

You can bank on it.

HARD STARES

To stare hard at things is to regain lost objects;
triumph over the glazed eye.

Granite.

Fine grains of concrete vision. Eyes
are buried in this bed of rock.
History is sunk here.

Chain-links of coloured shale,
dumped shells are what you must stare
through. Clay ribbed like the modern
block.

Rough looks pierce layers of textures. Painted
truths peel like your chafing skin. Pure
stone.

Sand: myriad of holes surface like your toast
fixed taut by an electrical flame. Under

the burden of hard stares everything
collapses. You see the fine cracks in love;
the crevices in ideas. Feel the hair-line fractures
of your faith
and the glaring need for manners.

ABSENCE

How crumpled your clothes look;
soiled and dishevelled
yet suggesting in their lilt
against the basket – something of you;
your damp intimate essentials.

Soiled clothes say more than
words. It's you there thrown
aside –
temporarily disembowelled;
drooping.

Then comes the hanging
from the clothes line, after
being placed in a wringer.

Frayed, your clothes suggest
you are coming to an end.

You have truly suffered. Let me
put my hand in those spaces –
the holes you have vacated.

Slowly,
you resurrect every Sunday
when your week's washing is dry.

HOUSEWORK

Blue Basin at the end of the track.
Cold. A wheel ground to a halt.
Taxis heading for Patna, time
heading for ruin,

and meteorologists waiting for the wet season.

But there is much to be done around
the house. Today, the grass must be cut,
gathered into my arms and dumped under
some banana trees:

there to rot as fertilizer,

if the chickens next door don't get it
first. There is also the car to fix. The
engine died last night; the carburettor

flooded like the street.

Nothing starts. Quarrels peter out. The garbage
is wet; it won't burn. Photos of my wife
are to be taken. Taxes to be paid; scripts to be marked.

It's late now; civilization has taken a tumble. Fine
rain sieves through my hands. I'll join the chickens
in raking in the compost.

SHEETS

Rent;
torn, bare and split like relationships
down the middle; these are your essentials —
sheets.

After years of usage it's like your
marriage — frayed at the edges
from too much careful handling.

You can look through the gaps to
the bottom of things. These are peep-
holes of discomfort.

More lies have coupled here than
meets the eye. You may soon have
to put the *Daily News*

to bed here. Those lines won't cover
everything.
These are unfriendly times.

DOWNSTAIRS

Downstairs is where we keep things that soon harden into rust:
old Klim pans full of nails, bolts, door hinges;
rodent-gnawed felt hammers of a German-made piano,
a broken clay jar and half-empty soft drink cases
with bottles encased in dust.

Downstairs cobwebs snare
unwary eyes; bricks, sand and lumber wait on you
hand and foot. Propped against six feet of raw earth
is a spade without a handle. To the left of this is
an English typewriter frozen in dirt, its keys bent on destruction,
the lone relic of Mother's adventure as a stenographer in town,
before it finally learnt the short hand of modernity.
Close by are huge ice tongs, their jaws fixed in air,
the only remnants of the shop Grandad ran before his heart
collapsed with the depression years. Everything is on ice here.

Further in, a wooden man with a broken hand for letters
                                        (Uncle Dan
made him) stares piercingly at you out of the darkness.
Uncle Dan was a cabinet maker who gave that up to work
with the Railway and then the Bus Company. His man still journeys
downstairs on his one leg, waiting for life's postman.

In this damp fortress
the past hatches its own memories among two abandoned
hen houses, a baby's crib and discoloured lizard's eggs.
Across a mound of rubble a ladder climbs to its own heights
while a pitch fork is lodged in the brain of an old head-piece.
There is also a bicycle frame, suspended from the low ceiling,
still peddling backwards to the age of Raleigh.
Fungus grows on old unstuck Italian-made shoes. Lately
a withdrawn broken night-chair has gone to France
though it supports a fibre mattress.

153

The whole fabric of society is here. Everything.
There is Germany's giant oven, the one that made the best
bread in the forties North-East of the East Dry River.
Seeing it I remember that Mammy – as her children and
grandchildren called her – took to baking after Papa,
her husband, died. Before that she worked in Panama.
A good Bajan woman, the symbol of her work ethic is now
broken, buried in sand near an overturned oil drum Dad
once brought home from the Shell tanker, *MV Martina*
or maybe it was the *MV Point Fortin*.

An extension cord creeps under the boards and wires
                                        it's way rather
reluctantly upwards. I live below (temporarily) and it's my link
with civilization. Recovering from nervous exhaustion,
levelled by junk and objects that define upstairs,
I, a rusting dog-chain and crawling memory hold
                                        downstairs together.

PLAYROOM

(for Sonia)

Here everything that your daughter owns
is collected in cardboard boxes.

Raggedy Ann, bent and broken groans
in the half-light; the sharp teeth of foxes

bare down on two copies of *The Three Little Pigs*;
while a telephone rings near four Phantom Migs

her Uncle sent for Christmas. A cracked
doll strips with wanton abandon.

Plastic children link arms against the
advances of Mickey Mouse and the probing

eyes of a view-finder. Natty the bee
is shattered; she has ceased buzzing.

I must learn to find love, hi-jacked
among a rubble of fractured
parts;
it's an art my daughter teaches daily.

PART II

THE GLARE HURTS

O minstrel galleons of Carib fire,
Bequeath us to no earthly shore until
Is answered in the vortex of our grave
The seal's wide spindrift gaze toward paradise.
— Hart Crane

NUMB

When a shower rips open its guts
fiercely, chopping loose from its moorings,
at dawn when the sun cuts

through to your figure
shut in from the numbing
pain that heralds another seizure

even as runnels drain the earth
of water
and frogs mutter at your bitter mirth,

beer-scented, lucid, comical, conceived
in the cracked mind of an outcast sailor
who traces with his finger or dead butts

an ashen path along a concrete
bannister that ants have crawled before;
it's 5.30 a.m. Wind. A broken bus beats its retreat

to the city. The sailor's dying; hear the bang of his door.

PA

in the quiet of the dining-room
an ageing man sits huddled over scrambled eggs;
a copy of the *Guardian* drooling from his hands.

And in the silent rage of his broken posture,
he concludes how seldom he laughed in those years when he had
sharp two-toned shoes, double-breasted suits and steady hands.

Blanks circle him;
and yet those days when he rolled and pitched
the seas with the best, are a memory away.

He muses how committed he was to the corner stones
of his world. Rocks that once supported a fixed drive.
He scrambles for his thoughts across the headlines

recounts on stubby fingers the vices he declined
the strain of sacrifice his children never held.

...But dazed by so much thought and recall
the ageing man keels over. Almost bent double, he's
anchored to his eggs.

AUNT

You used to make funny noises
in your throat and say it was
thunder; God talking to the
animals or rearranging his chairs;
then you would roll over and
play dead. It's more than twenty
years since they covered you with
flowers. You had no thunder in
your throat that day but you
played dead very well. God has
stopped talking to the animals and
his chairs are broken like a child's heart.

PATHWAY

(in memory of Mark)

Your heart stuttered from birth
and your little fist clenched life
for as long as you could – snatching
a handful of months.

You did in weeks what takes
some of us a life time; silently
lisping from cradle to grave.

Framed in your grey box, you posed
for your first real family photo;
stilled by the simple desire to look good.

A mat of dry grass sheltered
you from a hail of dirt
thrown by the world. Onlookers

worried about the location of your bed
of rock. You smiled off their concern
as your tiny arm cut a path-way

that they shall follow to that door.

ACCIDENT

That woman standing on the bridge
is desperate. Her thighs ache –
her faith is haemorrhaging. She will
thumb a lift – take

anything to get to the other side
of town. She will take that
approaching car.

Lights crash. Feel the hurt fender
of thigh; the eyes of head-lamps

gouged; the rage of twisted steering-
rack lodged in its can; torn bladder
of radiator leaks – the whole fractured
heap of metal is smashed.

A woman's time is aflame.

PAPER

That ball of paper has suffered its own accident.
It is entangled in its own crevices. Once a sheet that
snowed on this crust, it has been overtaken by
a hail of words. Twisted, it has taken a turn for the worse.

Lines criss cross and triangulate new positions. It
is wrapped in its own contours; transfixed by a quick
squeeze that a school boy has put on it. Close scrutiny
takes your eyes around the cancelled map; the ashes
of the fiery ring that hooped the abandoned exercise
labelled "Volcanoes".

Now a bin yawns wide to receive a world.

PART III

THE EYE EXPLODES

Come, fix upon me that accusing eye.
I thirst for accusation.

— W.B. Yeats

JUDGE DREADWORD

I am a murderer; I wring words by the rough of their necks.
I misplace commas and abuse silent W's. I use folk-
lift to get from one idea to the next.

I stab thoughts at people without
first preparing them by word of mouth.
I have language in a vice all my own. But today,
I appear before the country's chief judge and word protector:

Judge Dreadword. Yes I. Confess your atrocious crimes
to this Word Court. I am Judge Dreadword – I don't
brook silence in my court.

You are accused of lynching the word 'money' by
its second syllable; you violated a full-stop, you
stabbed three vowels when they weren't

looking. You exploded a bomb in the face of two
young phonemes. You copulated with the letters P and Y
…these acts make me blue

with rage, and I'm a hard man. I deal with your kind
every day. How do you plead Rude boy Q?
Guilty or not guilty? What should I do?

Not guilty sir. Take four hundred years. We must rid
society of your kind – insensitive word merchants like you
must be punished. You have no tradition, no lineage, no big

models. Don't write in this court, Take another two
hundred years. Rude boy Q, have you heard of Johnson,
Cavafy, Eliot, Whitman, Lorca, Pasternak, Mandelstam?

Li Po? No your Dreadness. I thought so; a mere literary shim-sham.
Don't cry. This court is a, product of a proven tradition
of oil and its related cultural benefactors –

BP, CIA, IMF, IOU, the UN, PNM – letters that matter
in the world. You want to destroy all that? Hush up.
I hear you detractors harbour vile thoughts against

foreign socio-linguists and visiting psycho-linguists you
draw crude lop-side effigies of Chomsky, you hunt and burn
the manifestos of British dialectologists and American politicians.

You dare to write letters to the press. Don't interrupt!
I heard you were tough, but you snivel in my court.
Take another four hundred years. How dare you corrupt

our language? Why don't you dot your i's? Don't talk. I
do all the talking here. This is my court. Leave me.
Court is adjourned. Nail him to the cross of a T.

SHOP

Buzzing voices crying for Koo
drown the broken wind in the corner.
Lard. 4lb rice

two pound sugar. No salt this week.
Chop. Meat swings in the balance. A pig
raises his trotter for silence.

Mark all this on the account. Koo
does not trust the rumours of
prosperity. He too has his little
red book. His sabots have the sharp
clipped alertness of the march-song
of high finance.

One night Koo out off with the turn
of his Yale locks. Ram got wind of it.
The shop is now under new management.

The proud sign goes up – VEGETABLE DEPOT –
R. Rampersad. (No Credit).
Things aren't clearly priced.
Koo is in Toronto now;
and the Depot seldom has vegetables.

Lard; life dread.

COUP OR THE HOPELESS ART OF WRITING

There is a fatal lethal flame
that burns old people's homes, houses,
stores, private enterprise and
public faith. Coups here are
as noisy as my caged pigeons.

There are more military juntas
than Caribbean experts on
international relations.

To sit and write this down
may seem a luxury to many. In plain
truth there is a coup to film
or stop or report. If I drop all
this and race ahead to

where the action is, I may
get there before the B.B.C.
correspondent – or the political
reporter for the *Washington Post*.

I could land a story before
the Mafia's next flight of ganja
takes off for Miami. I may even get
lucky and beat the C.I.A. to the punch;
burn with rage and stage the coup myself.

FOOTFALLS

(In memory of Walter Rodney)

In the precincts of this prison all is clear blue sky.
Action is what is left. Politicians can have the rest.

History is not found in history books.
It is the here and now – meaningful departure –
if it comes to that.

News time;
a nation footfalls down waterfalls of silence.

A blast is coming; it will not catch me unawares.
Ogun is not afraid of fire; he uses it.
Sigidi!

A dictator is turning to ashes in his chair
while trying to out stare
both a camera
and the sad truth of murder.

Note: *Sigidi*! – Shaka's war-cry. The song of the spear-blade as it
bites: I have eaten!

TAKING ORDERS

That soldier training in
the hills will shoot
his own reflection if

his commander orders it.
He drowses over his
butt. He longs to

turn to stone, to
be a living monument
to his people. He

will stare from the
heights of some cenotaph
at a museum of

lost artifacts, bones, shells
and shell-shocked men.

Bush clouds his farthest vision.
Attention!
He stiffens as he
realises his dream.

A PRIME MINISTER'S ADDRESS

There has been a marked increase in food production
and political violence. I continue to work.
There are forests to be cleared,
canals, dams and roads to be built;
borders to guard. These things take time;
an iron will.

A huge vision corrupts, when the race is against time.
Bauxite makes money – but it eats into
our human resources; Hydro power
means money

but it explodes into the green of greed
the need to get there ahead
of the next race.

Now all I have left are my guards
who regard the guards;
(They too have a destiny to mould)
a helicopter that flies behind
the iron stares of the people;
men's opinions when I give it to them;

and regular blackouts
when they see the whites of my eyes.

GENESIS OF THE CLOWNS

fates and freedoms
mariners and renegades
having a whale of a time

the stilled eye of the globe
the river of time shifts its bed to
dance a riot of colour

up river
there is a bend all right

A waterfall of
currencies
still dances on stilts

money, politics
and water rats
painting the country red

return backwards through the Word.

A *Reconnaissance* sails down its bed of limestone.
In that reburial – genesis.

PART IV

CAST A COLD EYE

Watching snow cover the ground, cover itself,
cover everything that is not you, you see
...the burial
of sleep, the down of winter, the negative of night.
— Mark Strand

SEVERITY

Love that pretends admiration must be blinded.
No. Shoot it first; nail it on the door of your mind
and let your bullets splatter it across the town.

Every poet is a wanted man; stay from your cave on the hill
and pick them off like the flies they are. Life is a
mean quick draw, it will kill you at high noon
and leave you for the circling crows. Stab

all those who say they come to help; turn your back on
the smiling agents of change; brand them with an X of disgust.
Let them swing from the fork of themselves.

That ringed helping hand offering a warm bed and a hot night-cap
must be slashed. That TV commentator shaking her head
in fake understanding must hear the trap-door fly.

That child's scream must be silenced. That steelband's incessant
music must be buried under the rubble of your thoughts. Your
neighbour's quarrels must be short-circuited along with their
deranged stereo.

In the dead of night,
you alone must be working at fever pitch.
That reflection that greets you in the morning must be shaved off
and re-examined.

All shadows must be electrocuted by your will
leaving you free to ride into the forest of paper,
alone.

TONIGHT'S NEWS

Rock bottom flints of memory.
The spinal stillness of the past.
No one is selling mangoes here.

The light is dim. The presenter is not
in focus. In fact there are no people there.
Nothing. It is now dark in this cave.

There are drawings on the wall.
The signs of the times. The future
is beneath this sheet. Stare.

Suddenly,
a gospel singer screams from the dust jacket of her disc

right past my future.

CALM

A calm is settling on him again; he is dead-
beat
a chill is leaving the room slowly.
His fever has broken.

Night is finished –
for now.

He stops staring at pools of silence.
It was not the final night;
just a breaker tripping off
a temporary breakdown.

Automatically,
he jumps as his Furelect shoots
the morning toast at his head.

GORDON ROHLEHR

"THESE COLLAPSING TIMES": REMEMBERING Q

I: INTRODUCTION

Victor Questel was born on 20th January, 1949 and died on 19th April, 1982. Named heroically Victor, David and Eric, Questel was invested with the hopes of his parents and grandparents that he would overcome the obstacles, slay the giants and like Eric Williams, the acclaimed "father of the nation" of Trinidad and Tobago, achieve greatness and maybe lead his people into the new world. Victor would have laughed at the notion of himself as conqueror of anything. Some of his most piercing perceptions derided the pretensions of Caribbean leaders to omnipotence and lamented the impotence of the younger generation of rebels to effect any significant transformation of the moribund old world they had inherited.

He wasn't and did not seek to be victor or conqueror of anything, except, perhaps, words that could either erupt wildly as if possessed, or withdraw into their own impregnable silence. The nearest he came to acknowledging the five round, smooth stones of his namesake, David the shepherd boy, was in his last collection of poems, *Hard Stares*, where stones are not weapons against the Goliaths of his post-colonial time, as they are in Kamau Brathwaite's "Negus,"[1] but emblems of the opacity and otherness of the world and the futility of his own efforts to stare beyond the blank, neuter and indifferent surfaces of things. The enemy of the first David was both visible and vulnerable: Questel's enemy was existential and lay both within himself and in the very otherness of phenomena.

As for the challenge that confronted Questel to grow into his third name, Eric, he never used it. Writing between 1969 and 1982, he intuited the implosion of the world that Williams and other patriarchs of first the West Indian Federation and newly independent Caribbean nations had striven to bring into existence. In Questel's play, *The Doctor He Dead,* 'Williams' is presented satirically as Eustace, Bill, and De

Doctor, three contradictory facets of a psychiatrist who can heal neither his own divided psyche, nor the deranged youth of Port of Spain frightened by all the concrete of the city.[2] Questel's only resemblance to Eric Williams lay in his intense quest – the mission suggested by his surname – for intellectual excellence, which culminated in his achievement of the first PhD in Literature to have been done at the University of the West Indies, St. Augustine, Trinidad and Tobago. The year was 1980 and Questel was a relatively young thirty-one years.

Yet, he at times presented himself as a failure and disappointment to ancestors who had hoped for more from him. Questel in his turn had little faith in the world that Eric Williams tried to create, or in the aspiration and the uncertainty of a transitional generation that, in the imagery of Roger McTair, Questel's fellow-poet, mistrusted both the road behind and the road ahead, even as it sought its direction through a lens of alcohol at corners and crossroads that had no visible signs pointing towards the future.[3]

To McTair's bewildered protagonists groping for direction at cross-roads, Questel added the figure of a spiritual vagrant who traversed an external and interior landscape of arbitrary and incongruous signs as he journeyed towards a destination that might be unrelated to earlier phases of the trip. Questel's dislocated protagonist was a mask through which he clinically and with courage and terror confronted his own condition: a seemingly inherited schizophrenia that he tried simultaneously to understand, control and even exploit, and conversely to conceal, disguise and evade. His major method for dealing with his condition was a mordant humour that was directed as much against himself as against the social situation and the circus of characters he caricatured. All of his "actors", his "clowns", whether portrayed with withering sarcasm or a sparing empathy, are what Lamming would have termed "Natives of [his] person" – that is, projections of Questel's deeply divided mind.

The divisions were many and extreme. For instance, there was the aforementioned gap between an external reality of perceived phenomena and a consciousness that vainly tried to impose coherence on an external world that was "other" and alien. An example of this gap is the poem "Linkages" where the images are disconnected from each other and contrary to the poem's title, serve as signposts in a journey that leads nowhere.

At the same time, Questel's real concern is not with the journey through the landscape, but with his own obsessions of love, sex, doubt and faith, all of which manifest a common meaninglessness. The Sartrean strangeness of the external landscape does not reflect, but is an omen of the strangeness of the interior one where all things are strange and disconnected from each other.

Questel at times portrays himself as a comical cartoon-like character, confined by or entrapped in the frames or lines that are drawn by some controlling mind: a Comic Artist who is, perhaps, God as supreme cartoonist and manipulator of empty shapes that play at absurd games of power and control. Here, the division is between the designs of the human will and those of some superior controlling agency unnamed in Questel's poetry.

There is also the division between the conflicting religions of Questel's forebears who were Anglicans on one side and Shouter Baptists on the other. Questel finds himself in a gap, or what he terms a "blank" where he twists in agnostic denial of the Afro-Saxon sectarianism of the Anglicans, but never quite embraces the kinetic theatre of energy and spirit possession of the Spiritual Baptist faith. While the Spiritual Baptists in *Near Mourning Ground,* the central and centring book of this collection, seemed to offer Questel a possible pathway into an alter/native aesthetic to existentialist Absurdism that he as a 1970's intellectual found attractive, he remained a child of his time, sometimes cheerfully, sometimes morbidly dislocated from all systems. He deeply doubted that bridging the aesthetic divide between the "African" and the "Saxon" halves of his existence would help heal the fissures in his mind. He nevertheless did try to bridge the gap he perceived within himself and to explore the possibility of self-healing.

His addiction to wordplay reflected his recognition of the various and complex dimensions of dividedness. The pun, for example, offered words or word-fragments linked by sound but of diverse meaning. With the pun, words became free agents with an apparent will of their own. The pun was a false link; a celebration and mockery of the disconnectedness of things. The pun offered the poet power to access simultaneously double and triple meanings and create his own illusory universe within and against the "blank" that stretched beyond the safety of muttered or loudly articulated creeds. The pun wasn't the only device he employed. There were fewer puns as mirth and acrid laughter at self and circumstance became less possible towards the end. But Questel never abandoned punning.

In his journey towards autonomy of voice, Questel both sought out and fought against the power of the dominant Muses, the ancestor-poets of the diasporan Caribbean naissance. In Questel's case, these ancestor-poets were mainly Derek Walcott and Kamau Brathwaite. Questel was ambivalent in his response to Walcott. As a researcher for the PhD on Walcott, he cross-catalogued over five hundred of Walcott's polemical essays and articles, his "hack's hired prose"[4] or, as Questel jestingly termed them, his "axe, ired, pose."[5] Beneath the mask of irreverence, Questel patterned himself on Walcott and, for a decade, functioned as a steady commentator on matters literary and cultural, as Walcott had been during the 1960s.

His doctoral thesis on Walcott was the most comprehensive pioneer research done on that author. It occupied the years of the mid to late 1970s, that is, the middle years of Questel's quest for voice, vision and coherence. His encounter with the mercurial Walcott confirmed his insight into his own dividedness, but not into the possibility of a healing reconciliation. Significantly, the title of Questel's thesis was: "Paradox, Inconsistency, Ambivalence and Their Resolution in Derek Walcott's Writings 1946-1975". He was exploring through his readings of Walcott's life and writing the very elements that bothered him in his own.

Questel also listened critically to the equally compelling voice of Kamau Brathwaite who at the time was recognized as Muse and spirit-guide into all sorts of wildernesses: Afro-Caribbean, Afro-American, African. It was Brathwaite's protagonist in "Negus" who sought both "the stone that would confound the void"[6] and the trickster tongues of both Grecian Ulysses and West African Anansi, whose words could "blind your god".[7] Brathwaite, an experimenting, improvising writer, seemed to offer endless trailways toward an alter/native tradition to the Euro-Modernist little-ease in which Questel was entrapped. Questel imitated aspects of Brathwaite's style – the punning, broken lines, word-echoing and tendency towards journey-narrative – though he realized from early that he had to find his own voice through processes that would require rebellion against the ancestor-Muse.

Nonetheless, in his calm moments, he acknowledged the importance of pathfinders. In "Lines", a poem dedicated to St. Lucian poet Robert Lee, he advised his fellow-neophyte to pay attention to the pathfinders while cutting his own pathway into "the bush".[8]

Apart from Walcott and Brathwaite, Questel read and wrote poems that alluded to the work of several other West Indian writers. Lamming, Harris, Naipaul, Ladoo, Leroi Clarke, the painter and poet, all contributed to his shaping of his own voice These were all intensely committed writers whose ongoing work made Questel realise that he was not alone in his mission, whatever that mission was or turned out to be. Conversely, he was profoundly alone in his journey through his own private dark thicket of nightmares: the tangle and fissures of his own wilderness, the emptiness of his own "blank"; the terror of "Nothing" that could at once seem to be profound and trivial; the impenetrable opacity of things, the uncontrollable arbitrariness of experience.

Beneath all this lay the terror he faced of "cracking-up". Much of his laughter grew out of fear, for he saw his situation in the characters he portrayed, some with apparent mockery: for example, the figure of Shaka and his rhetorical quest for freedom; or the captain of the rusting *Federal Maple* in "Sea Blast" who continues to chart his ship's course to nowhere; or Lamont, the genteel madman of "Lament", or Questel's father, a retired amnesiac sailor in whose dementia Questel read his own future; or his uncle Simeon who vainly tries through his not-too-hot gospelling to turn the lost young pan men of Crossfire from their doomed mission of fratricidal gang warfare. He portrayed his fear through simple images: a coconut shell cracked across the third eye; a schoolboy's crumpled geography test; a pop-up toaster – investing ordinary objects with primordial significance. One of his ancestral guides is Zanda, an architect and kaiso-jazz pianist whom Questel in "Triangles of Sound" presents as a hump-backed Legba-figure whose exploratory blending of Calypso melodies with Jazz harmonies suggests a possibility for reconciling ancestral cultural bloodlines, a triangulation of cultures created by and now redeeming the Triangular Trade that once engendered post-Columbian Caribbean societies and their common dilemma of diverse ancestors at war still in the blood of today's people. Such reconciliation, however, is only temporary and does not outlive the moment of performance.

In the end, there are more questions than answers, journeys than arrivals, beginnings than meaningful conclusions. The fear engenders then overclouds laughter; the fissures persist or remain possible; descent into black cave of the psyche reveals only shards of dumb rock. The world gazed at and the gaze itself remain hard, unremitting, severe and separate beyond reconciliation.

II: PRELUDE

Prelude consists of the twenty poems that Questel published in *Score* (1972)[9], a collection that contained a score of poems by each of two poets: Anson Gonzalez and Victor Questel. "Prelude", the first poem of *Victor Questel: Collected Poems*, was first written and revised in 1971, the year of Questel's graduation from UWI, St Augustine and his first year (September 1971-July 1972) as English and History teacher at St Stephen's College, Princes Town. The heyday of Black Power (1969-1970) had come and gone. Questel, an aspiring writer, was in the process of accumulating images and impressions as he shuttled to and fro between urban Port of Spain and the canefields of the Central range. This journey involved movement between the major ethnic communities of North and Central Trinidad and presented Questel with his first real vision of the variety of communities and cultural situations that might be included in the name "Trinidadian".

(1)

"Prelude", a clear imitation of "Prelude," the opening poem of Derek Walcott's *In a Green Night: Poems 1948-1960*[10] is Questel's first poem of self-location in the turbulent ethos of his time. Its opening lines made reviewer, the poet, playwright and journalist Eric Roach, wince at the forced puns that were to become Questel's trademark.

> On receiving my indenture
> I bit into the future
> and chewed the past

On close consideration, the lines yield meaning. Freedom, whether African Emancipation (1834) or the end of East Indian Indentureship. (1917) offers the appetizing prospect of a future, a life to be chewed and savoured with new false teeth. But freedom has brought no true release from certain types of servitude. It has been a circling back to the past, or a forward lurch into new forms of oppression.

Questel, on contemplating the recent defeat of what has been termed the Black Power "Revolution" through the sceptical eyes of the children of Asiatic indentureship, is confronted with a vision of cyclic repetition, something similar to East African *zamani* where time and history are perceived as cyclic and the future is the past. In "Prelude", the past offers

186

images of primal tragedy signified by the allusion to Kerbala, the death of the Prophet's grandsons and the Shiite ceremony of remembrance, Hosein/Hossay, still practised in Trinidad. The past is:

> tajas of crematoriums
> where
> skulls sulk at the
> extending bones
> dancing the moon

The tajas/tazias are the elaborate and beautiful "tombs" of the Prophet's grandsons, Hosein and Hassan, rendered in papier-maché over bamboo frames; and though Muslims in Trinidad bury rather than cremate their dead, these tazias are burnt at the sea's brink after the Hossay/Hosein ceremony of street-dancing ("dancing the moon"). The image of skulls sulking at scarecrow-like skeletons ("extending bones"), suggests that even after thirteen centuries – (the Battle of Kerbala occurred on October 10, 680 AD) – the fratricidal hatred of the original confrontation has not abated. There has been no reconciliation or forgiveness and consequently no laying to rest of the calamitous past.

The sulking skulls can also mean that the ancestors resent the degraded rituals by which their current descendants remember them. The diasporan late twentieth century protagonist – here Islamic, but by extension and analogy, Afro-Creole – is trapped in the vision of a Nietzschean eternal recurrence of past betrayal and fratricide, or of commemoration as perversion and violation.

Travelling from South to North along what used to be the Princess Margaret Highway, later to be known as the Sir Solomon Hochoy Highway, Questel recognizes that the journey offers varying omens of the skeleton, the most startling of which is not the discarded burnt frame of the taja, but the empty billboard:

> And here
> a skeleton-frame of a
> bill-board
> hawks
> the profundity of nothing

"Here" is the commercialized present, a space dominated by hawks whose rituals and music are absolutely different from those of the

Hosein dancers. Generally, their space is filled with advertisement, but this billboard is an empty frame devoid of portrait or exhortation, signifying a nation driven by commerce but devoid of identity or voice. The billboard's rectangular frame of lines enclosing nothing will recur in Questel as the empty lines framing a cartoon in which he is confined by the Creator as cartoon artist, or as an image of the void or the "blank" in which he finds himself trapped.

The next image in this South to North journey is that of the burning rubbish-heap, the La Basse, which in 1971 sent a thick pall of stinking smoke over Port of Spain and into the Northern Range. The burning dump that heralded triumphal entry into the nation's capital became the central motif in Naipaul's *Guerillas*[11] where it functioned as a Dantesque or Conradian image of the circles of the Inferno. "It sits like lead on my soul," Naipaul declared in 1971.

Questel's La Basse is almost romantic. It "quietly exhales smoke the colour / of a glow -/worm," by whose wan illumination the poet finds his way to the "cross/roads of creation." Here at Legba's or Christ's "crossroads" he identifies himself deprecatingly as a journeyman writer:

> caught between the hollow knees of my existence
> blinded by scan-
> sions s-pewing
> my alter-
> ing moods
> at the cross
> roads of creation
> I write
> doggedly, like a cur.

This self-portrait is over-severe. He perceives his writing as an act of masturbation, driven, compulsive, answering a desperate immediate need – but not the real thing. His "masturbation" climaxes in nothing like Wordsworth's "spontaneous overflow of powerful feeling", but rather is a wretched, dogged self-induced "spew" of random moods. The agonized twisting of words – 's-pewing', 'alter', 'cross' – suggests that Questel saw himself as one driven to make Stephen Dedalus's choice between religious faith, (pew, altar, cross) and that unknown universe beyond the approved limits of religion.

The poem ends with images of both implosion ("frenzy turning inwards") and entrapment, the latter of which had become an island-trope that had appeared before in the Crusoe / Castaway poems of both Derek Walcott,[12] and Eric Roach[13] and most elaborately in the "zoo" poems of Kamau Brathwaite.[14] A common feature of these ancestor poems is the loneliness of the entrapped protagonist who may glimpse limitless horizons but cannot travel beyond the edges of his confining island. Arriving early at a similar vision, Questel portrays himself as:

> trapped by the webbed
> horizons weaved
> by rainbows

Acknowledging, without really surrendering to the limitations of the island's cage, the narrator says:

> I become a tiger
> and stalk my stripes
> of coloured solitude

Questel first endeavours to turn his gaze away from the rainbow-vapoured illusions of the horizon's web of light and colour, towards a bleak recognition of the island's cage which he simultaneously acknowledges and resists. This image of the poet as castaway and caged cat could have been suggested by Brathwaite's portrait in *Islands* of the caged leopard who "burns, and paces/ turns again and paces," an icon of defiant rage and frustration. Brathwaite's leopard, like Questel's tiger, inhabits a narrow cage within his island's greater cage. He is

> caught... in this care
> ful cage of glint, rock,
>
> water ringing the islands'
> doubt[15]

If Brathwaite's 'leopard' retains a glimmering hope of liberation, Questel's 'tiger', having already witnessed the failure of the 1970 February Revolution, has no such hope. All that remains for him is his cage, his solitude and his instinctive but futile stalking, his secretive pursuit of prey visible only to himself. The words "stripes" and "coloured" both suggest that the tiger's dilemma is one of mixed or variegated heritages, the perspective of mulattitude which, after the apparent collapse of an ideology of neo-Garveyism, was being heavily endorsed by Questel's ancestor-Muse, Derek Walcott.[16] "Stripes", however, apart from suggesting dual heritages or non-heritages, also evokes a history of castigation – as in "beaten with many stripes" – that is similar to the remembered scars of African enslavement.

Questel was at the beginning of his journey towards becoming a writer, confronted by the challenge of whether to start from memory or, as Walcott was then advocating, amnesia. In "Prelude", memory first appears as the Hosein festival, a fixed commemoration of "the founding murder" which, according to Rene Girard, marks the inscriptive moment of young religions.[17] By the end of the poem, "memory" produces a vision of parallel cages of unredeemed or unexorcised pain. Faced with a dilemma of choosing similar to Walcott's, Questel, as he approaches "the cross/roads of creation" defines himself in "Fragment of a Letter Two" as "outsider, outrider, doubter." As outrider, he functions as a warner, a foreseer of obstacles, much more than a clearer of the royal way for Eric's passage or Shaka's. As outsider he tries to hold himself aloof from a protest movement whose vision and message have "harden[ed] to marble", that is, become rigid, doctrinaire and dead. As doubter he traverses "this bull-ring of solitude", which is simultaneously a public theatre of brutal contestation, and an interior space of constant and violent self-confrontation where bull and matador are the same person and the protagonist is driven out of his solitude towards the acceptance of a public creed – "gored to a public faith".

(2)
"Pan Drama"

In Questel's ongoing journey towards becoming a poet, these roles of outsider, outrider, doubter and deeply wounded matador are interchangeable. Most frequently though, he functions as outsider, witness, half-committed commentator on the shifting life-stream of people and objects that flow across his lens. In "Pan Drama", he stands outside of yet empathises with the Panman who, his moment in the Carnival masquerade over, still has to "push on" as he helps wheel his band homewards. Questel's narrator recognizes Mas as a transient phenomenon but declares an affinity with the Panman, the protagonist who endures after the festival is over and the stage reverts to its pristine emptiness. "Pan

Drama" seeks to explore Mas and Pan as major metaphors in a theatre of secular ritual that annually absorbs, consumes and disgorges multitudes of players back into the tedium of ordinary reality.

The narrator, who is neither Masman nor Panman, but someone like the Bookman of the Devil Band, who comes at the end of the masquerade and chronicles the procession of souls on their way out of the masquerade of life and towards "Death's other kingdom",[18] is, in his quest for meaning, far more emotionally involved in the phenomena he seeks to interpret than the impassive, indifferent Bookman. So he begins by confessing his empathy with the Panman.

> Ex-
> it
> mas' man
> push on
> pan man
> a man
> attuned, trapped
>
> caught (like me)
> making
> subtle inden-
> tations
> in his
> spider web

The Panman who must "push on" is the man who after and without the illusionary uplift of music and mas' must press on with the ordeal of life within which he is "trapped" even as he affirms his attunement. What does this attunement/ entrapment dyad mean? Perhaps that he is in harmony with the silent ordeal and tedium of things beyond the masquerade's loud noises; or that some master tuner has, after heating and hammering his soul, set him in tune with the melody of life, or entrapped him beyond his willed acquiescence in the spider's web of existence. We will return to these speculations when we consider the ending of the poem.

The poet next reflects on what has happened to Pan and its makers in the process of the steel band's being manipulated by the image-makers of the new national culture

(now)
limbo-
ing from flambeau-
pan-yard
to
flying Pan Am

a-
massing cultural
missions

The cultural commissars have now – (that is, after the Black Power
awakening of 1970) – relocated the limbo, the old-time gayelle of the
flambeau-lit pan-yard, whose descendant was the ritualised space of the
stickfighting kalinda yards, in their schema for the cosmeticized redefi-
nition of national culture. The 'yard-culture' of the black underground
has received a face-lift, and the Panman has been redefined from bad
john, criminal, gangster, shiftless idler, to "cultural ambassador" . In the
process of such transformation, he has made a gigantic leap from the
spraddled, horizontal and grounded posture of the limbo dancer to that
of the high-flying, world-travelling cultural missionary. There is a nice
wordplay here – a "subtle indentation", one guesses – on Pan Am/
Panman. Pan American Airways (while it yet existed) was a major
sponsor of the Pan Am North Stars steel orchestra and, like all other
commercial sponsors of Pan, part of the bourgeois pacification process
of both Mas and Pan; part of the cooling, the taming, the trapping and
tuning of the peri-urban underclass; part too of the general
commoditization and Americanization of all that used to be "folk" or
"national" in both consciousness and culture.

The captain and tuner of Pan Am North Stars, the great Anthony
Williams, was one of the finest pan-makers, inventors and tuners of his
time, and may even be **the** Panman that the narrator tells "push on", and
with whom the narrator empathises, even as he accepts and holds him
up as symbol. Anthony Williams was to grow reclusive and depressed –
a metaphor of the situation of the artist in post-colonial, post-Independ-
ence Trinidad and Tobago; a metaphor, indeed, of the true state of the
nation beneath and beyond the mask promoted in tourism brochures.
Pan American Airways would suffer a near fatal breakdown in the 1980s.

There are other dimensions in Pan and the Pan Man:

> (then)
> bombing down
> the town
> down

> Frederick Street
> to the chipping feet
> featly Jouvert
> morning

This is both an allusion to the "Bomb tune", which was usually a light classical melody set to the Calypso rhythm, practised in secret by each major steelband and released on Jouvert morning. Here was, simultaneously, the bourgeoisification of grassroots consciousness and the calibanization of classical high culture: the ambivalent aspects of colonial Afro-Saxon assimilationism. So one has Jouvert masqueraders emerging from Port of Spain's demi-monde and, without contradiction, joining a teeming black and coloured middle class in chipping "featly". The word "featly" is derived from Ariel's song in Shakespeare's *The Tempest* ("Come Unto These Yellow Sands"), where the dancers are instructed to kiss, curtsy and "foot it featly" to a chorus sung by "sweet sprites" against a background of barnyard noises – barking dogs, crowing cocks and the like.

Questel juxtaposes two bizarre moments of cultural transgression – Shakespeare's Seventeenth Century marriage of aristocratic and pastoral/ bucolic forms and Trinidad's carnivalesque melding of underclass breakaway "wuk-up" with pseudo-aristocratic dainty mas, characterised more by the "chip" than by belly-rolling or waist-jukking wine-down.

Beneath this already complex masquerade of rhythms and dance performance styles, lurks a sinister and only partially suppressed reality. The "bombing down" of the city's centre is an allusion to the 1970 February "Revolution" and the turbulence of the Black and powerless decades before 1970. These were the flambeau, limbo, panyard, Hellyard men who created the culture now under appropriation by the national commissars. The words:

> Wheeling across
> the whole

193

are a recognition of how Pan and Mas have become accepted by all levels of society as iconically "national". Yet "wheeling across" suggests uncertainty, delirium, the staggering movement of a society temporarily or maybe permanently intoxicated; the untrustworthiness of the consolatory slogans, "all awee is one," or "here every creed and race find an equal place."[19] For Hindu nationalists, then and now, the Steelband, limbo, Calypso and Carnival, were no more than Creole/non Indian symbols that were being imposed on them by successive "Black" governments, whose objective was the alienation and marginalization of "Hindus and Indians".

The narrator of "Pan Drama" next focuses on the stage upon which the Panman and his colleague the Calypsonian perform their inauthentic "folk" culture for both the local petty bourgeoisie and "colourless/ mocking folk from /far away smog/ lands," whose responses share the common quality of insincerity. The smile of the local gentry is "blurred"; the laughter of the colourless foreigners at whom the entire half-arsed performance is aimed, is "mocking". The content of the national folk song, those "calypso tunes /of/chamber pot drama/ or racial melodrama," is at times filthy. Alternatively, political commentary has become part of the ongoing melodrama of inter-ethnic quarrelling. The word "melodrama" suggests insincerity, exaggeration, falsity of feeling – for even the quarrels within and between ethnicities are, like everything else, faked and manipulated rituals: masquerade. The entire scenario – the actors, audience, performers and the material being performed – is crap, and sickens the narrator who is himself a kind of performer, trapped if attuned to the spider's web of stale sexuality, "armed only [with my] rubber-ended sticks."

The poem ends with the Panmen seen through the eyes of a handful of tourists who are attracted to a rootedness in the music that has somehow managed to survive the taming process – perhaps because the Panmen, despite the derogation of the narrator himself, have remained "attuned / to their/base tenor / of / living." The grand irony here is that while the local commissars of culture have been working hard to refine Pan and all other aspects of folk performance into a sterile but more daintily acceptable "brand", the tourists at whom this brand is being brandished are – even the most obtuse and innocent of them – more immediately responsive to the authenticity of the players who play their lives, in spite of the overlay of conditioning that has tried to govern their sound.

The narrator ends by reaffirming both the attunement to and entrapment in life that he shares with the Panman. He describes himself as he departs from the poem

> making subtle
> indentations
> in my
> spider web
>
> I wheel away

He now perceives himself not only as helplessly caught object and instrument of some greater harmonizing force external to him and larger than his will, but also as a secret agent who is subtly trying all the time either to escape from or impose his own etching on the spider's web within which he is trapped. Since the "spider web" was a major design in the tenor pan's evolution, the narrator may be affirming his own identity as a maker, a tuner, a subject simultaneously tuning and attuned, a Pan-creator and creature of a greater but still unidentifiable master force that has trapped and tuned him.

The final line, "I wheel away", evokes both the image of the now tired Panman pushing the wheeled frames of the steelband's skeleton back to the pan yard, and the image of an intoxicated reveller walking his wavering and circuitous pathway, not necessarily homeward to yard, but 'away' from the scene towards an indefinite future in which he is resolved to persist and endure.

(3)
"Down Beat"

"Down Beat" is, like "Pan Drama", a poem of self-signification , except for the fact that the narrator here defines himself in the anti-heroic/ heroic tones of the trickster, the small survivor who begins, like one of Beckett's tramps, with a listing of his possessions:

> A pocket
> myself an arse

a stick of grass
Pinching all to stay alive

One is immediately struck by the economy, the sparseness and the humour of this naming of parts. He pinches his pocket in the sense of cutting and contriving, living off the bare necessities, spending as little as possible. Or he may be telling us that he is a professional pickpocket. He pinches himself to stay alert to the trials of the turf. He pinches women's backsides because he is a sexual harasser; or he may be telling the reader of the intimate sexual contact that he has with his lover – real or imaginary – which gives him the will to stay alive and provides him with his soulful, jaunty strut. He also pinches his spliff of marijuana – his "stick of grass" – in the two senses of smoking as little as possible, or of rolling the ends of his improvised cigarette. All of this "pinching" is done "to stay alive". The narrator is a survivalist, living on few and mean resources, making ends meet.

Verbal economy, a complex wordplay of multilayered punning, rhyme, semi-rhyme, obscure allusion, bizarre combinations of ideas, and a jaunty, jazzy rhythm that is reflected in his nonchalant strut downtown to an incessant, inaudible beat: – these are the resources upon which legally, illegally and with a certain manufactured elation, he survives. Movement is a major element in his survival kit, whether it takes the form of his keen observation of the passage of events and images across the screen of his eye, or of his own seemingly aimless journey from where he lives on the border of everything and every place, to his "liming" stations scattered across the city. Movement is visibly illustrated by the words' aimless meander from side to side across the page. It is suggested by the present continuous tense in which the narrator tells his story, and by the transitory procession of unrelated images across the screen of the narrator's gaze – as if life were a slideshow of dissociated phenomena. Sometimes it is the narrator who is in motion, while the world around him is a blur. At other times the narrator is fixed in space, a trapped man and mind, while the world moves indifferently and "other", outside of his lens.

The name "Down Beat" suggests "beaten down", yet, located in a context of Jazz, it also connotes "cool" and "bluesy", dancing along with whatever life provides. *Downbeat* is the name of a magazine that focuses on Jazz and jazz-related musics. Questel's narrator seems to be morally neutral – or it may be that he never allows his mind's eye to focus on any particular phenomenon long enough for moral reflection. Thus Snake Eye's rape, last night's wake, carnival masquerade, political "demon / stration," work or rumour of available (i.e. temporary) labour, the ole mas of elections, the arcane rituals and rhetoric of cricket, are given equal measure and valuation in his apparently non-discriminating consciousness. Life is continuously on the move; Death hovers and can swoop at any moment. He watches them both, trapped in, part of, yet in consciousness apart from their dance. Yet, he cannot be dismissed as having no objective in life. His central objective is to survive and he assesses each situation – the wake, a death ceremony where there will be food, the fete where there will be drink – in terms of its potential for sustaining life.

Life itself is a gamble, like the romey/rummy hands he plays, his betting on horses, his faint hope of finding work in a context where no hands are ever wanted, or in the last resort, as one who is paid to hold a spot for some potential immigrant seeking a visa from the American Embassy in Marli Street. This is, in fact, the highest or lowest point in his situation as one whose profession is to wait, even though his strategy is to keep moving along with life. Here he waits in order to facilitate someone else's flight from the trap of a society where he is himself entrapped, and like the Panman of "Pan Drama", strangely attuned to its every whim and circumstance.

He bears each day's frustration with a kind of grace and with constant (merely verbal) performance: with masking, the pretence of being in control of circumstance, of being able – returning to the metaphor from "Pan Drama" – to make "subtle indentations" in the etched spider's web of the Maker's design. But at times the puns, jokes, scatological humour, sexual innuendos, marijuana reinforced by the equally illegal bush rum, prove insufficient to quell the pangs of hunger. At such junctures, he is forced to acknowledge (to himself, of course, since this entire confession is a monologue) that his mask of insouciance and his elation at being able to manipulate language have failed him, and he is reduced to "cursing dem all / forgetting it all," as his calypso-jazz soliloquy withers into truth and self-knowledge.

His final vision – despite a last attempt to reconstruct his macho image – is that he is a being ensnared in history, that his body still dances to the sun's strum and lash, still suffers under the sting of a slavery that has grown or has always been cosmic.

197

And overhead the sun strumming along
lashing along meh back
and I calling dat George
substituting half measures

for the w - hole

The sun "strumming along" overhead is a guitar-pan that keeps time
with the bass pulse of the pounding headache that he gets from drinking
bad rum and smoking marijuana on an empty stomach. At least part of
his continued enslavement to circumstances must lie in his own willed
choice of bad options. Neither bush rum nor marijuana would have been
free, yet our downbeat man spends his meagre, scraped-together
earnings on those two pain-numbing anodynes rather than on the food
he really needs.

Hungry both physically and mentally, broken in spirit, he is too
exhausted to fight against fixed cosmic design. So he lets go, resigns
himself to the scheme of things, while making a final effort at a sexual
pun: "w- whole". "W – hole" is the flattened ending of this soliloquy of
discordant word-notes. It suggests the fragmentation and incomplete-
ness of the protagonist's life; it reveals the void, hole or abyss that no sex,
real or imagined, can exorcise. It also hints the narrator has begun to
work his way back, towards grotesque optimism, the grim laughter by
which he has lived and confronted each day's absurd cycle of emptiness.
He can laugh at life, but he cannot wriggle out of the trap or climb out
of its hole.

(4)
"Tom"

"Tom" is the first of these poems from the early 1970s to treat with the
February Revolution of 1970, the most amazing phenomenon of Questel's
time; one from whose powerful vortex he tried to remain detached.
Adopting the persona of timid Tom, the man who seeks to avoid
engulfment in a revolution he watches from the margins, because he
fears betrayals he can foresee, Questel's "avuncular" narrator, a Tiresias
figure who has lived through recurrent cycles of historical unchange, has
no hope that 1970 can mean a way out of the trap of history.

Written in reaction to Kamau Brathwaite's reconstruction of Uncle

198

Tom in *Rights of Passage,* Questel's "Tom" begins by probing the vexed issue of who was more responsible for the grave wrong of slavery. Was it the European or African ancestor? This question had been raised before in Walcott's "A Far Cry from Africa" and "Ruins of a Great House",[20] but it had remained one of the huge, unanswerable questions of New World history and one of the traps entramelling post-Independence would-be architects of new postcolonial nations. Questel, answering his Muse, Brathwaite, declares the question irrelevant. All ancestors and their deeds have merged into a single error and cancel out each other.

> The wrong that are
> our ancestors
> square the deal.
>
> I have no grief
> for words to
> flounder upon

One notes that in an earlier version of the poem, "wrong" is rendered as "wrongs," which makes greater grammatical sense and leaves one to wonder whether the published version, "the wrong that are/our ancestors/square the deal" – is a misprint. Nevertheless, Questel's meaning is clear. If Walcott had in "Choc Bay"[21] stated that all a poet had or needed were "words to fling [his] griefs about," Questel claims here to have no grief. 1970 had "hammered out" all his dreams and fancies.[22]

Similarly, if Brathwaite's questing omawale, recovering from a devastating encounter with his shattered ancestral history declares hopefully:

> But the way lost
> is a way to be found
> again[23]

Questel's quester replies

> for the way lost
> is the way
> lost

Period. There can be no reconnection of blood lines, no rediscovery of Carpentier's "lost steps", no renewed contact with ancestors or the ancestral past. The only link, indeed, between past and present lies in the similarity of their failure and crippledom. So it is with dry sadness that Questel addresses the issue of Black Power and the February Revolution.

> and revolution
> is the scandal
> of poverty
> sandalled to the
> dust of processions.

Amazing words, these, suggesting a soul-wearying perception of all that rhetoric of 1970, all those feet, all those journeys, processions, marches reduced, ground to dust, wilderness of spirit, desert; even as the "scandal of poverty" remains society's enduring reality.

The haiku-like second section of "Tom" maintains and fills out the exhaustion of the first.

> Arches don't rise here
> though for some
> they fall with
> each step.

According to this perception, the Caribbean stage differs from that of historic Europe, Rome especially, whereas in France also, triumphal arches honoured the military achievements of each new crop of conquering Caesars. The absence of such monuments in the Caribbean has long been advanced as evidence of the region's lack of tradition, "a tiered concept of the past" as Walcott termed it in what in 1970 was the recently published essay: "What the Twilight Says: An Overture."[24] Questel amusingly reflects on this Afro-Saxon truism: no statues, monuments, triumphal arches, means no "history", "civilization", "tradition". Questel is saying that all of the great moments of militancy in the Caribbean have fallen flat, like the fallen arches of the feet of those who marched from February to April in 1970. Flatness, fallen arches, collapsed insteps, ruined feet: these are the signifiers of the great anti-climactic moment of 1970 – signifiers that become more distinct with every ongoing step the pilgrims take in this absurd journey.

Section iii is a series of riddles and riddling puns. It begins:

> To fashion consciousness

is
still to cut a figure,
yet another
pound of flesh

Were the leaders and ideologues of Black Power really fashioning – that is shaping, remaking, instilling in their followers – new and healthier ways of understanding or contemplating self or identity? Or were they capering, masquerading, jive-assing, designing costumes for the catwalk, cutting out paper dolls? "Cut a figure" leads to the idea of ghoulish sacrifice, of cutting "yet another /pound of flesh". "Yet another" indicates that other pounds of flesh have in the past been demanded of society's followers – the people, the proles, the masses beguiled by their new leaders' "gift of the grab". Questel's wordplay fuses "gab" – rhetoric, old talk, trivial conversation – with "grab". The end of today's rhetoric is tomorrow's predation.

Questel had as little faith in the new would-be leaders as he had in their predecessors. At the vast old age of twenty-five years, he had resigned himself to the role of detached observer, a Bookman recording the nation's procession towards foreseeable disaster, an Uncle Tom warning from the margin of society about the "triangular betrayals" that he foresees – the complex double- and triple-cross taking shape amidst a chorale of howling pot hounds.

His final image is one of offshore, oil-drilling platforms, the nation's ultimate reality, generating mineral wealth at the expense of potential ecological disaster: the ruin of pristine beaches with oil slick.

the oil-
slick of our shores

waves of survival
for the slickest

Being one of the world's oil producing nations gives the island a disproportionate stature and self-importance. There is glamour in the idea that such material wealth is available, as there is glamour in the rhetoric of the slick new leaders who have emerged to engineer the acquisition of this wealth. But the oil-derricks have their negative side – ecological pollution – just as the rhetoricians of the new nation have theirs – a capacity to betray, Anansi smartness, smoothness in self-

201

survival regardless of who or how many may suffer or have to surrender their pound of heart's flesh.

(5)
"Nelson Island Blues"

"Nelson Island Blues" is a poem about the isolation of some of the 1970 detainees and the secretive silence, the absence of news or even rumours of what was happening to the men detained. The detentions and the secret tribunals that followed were a strategy for collecting evidence to justify the incarceration of the Black Power leaders. The State detained first and then sought evidence in fruitless searches for arms, ammunition and subversive literature. Having sustained its spirit on rhetoric and the acclamation of crowds, Black Power was condemned to die in silence and isolation.

The poem begins with the words "one-eyed" because Nelson was a one-eyed slave plantation owner who wore a pirate's patch over the blinded eye. "One-eyed" also suggests that the threatened government had lost half of its vision in its choice of a state of emergency and the arbitrary detention of dissidents, and its attack on conversation and communication. Imprisonment on that island was an illustration of the central motifs of "castaway" and "trap" that Questel attributed to existence itself. Nelson Island had been a venue of confinement in the colonial past. Now it was emerging as a symbol of unchange less than a decade after Independence in a nation whose leader was deaf and nearly as blind as the great Caucasian ancestor.

The narrator, Questel's imagined detainee, who is a mask for Questel himself, reacts bitterly to the "grey monotony" of existence on that tiny island rock. It is a "Molotov monotony" because of the constant explosion of wave on rock and the fixed dream that runs through the head of the protagonist of destroying the city. There is an insane connection between the monotonous yet explosive landscape and the vision of blood and ashes that has now become fixed in his eyeballs. The imprisonment on Nelson Island engenders the very attitude and situation it was meant to prevent: "a foetus/future full of scars left." Detention, isolation, silence, entrapment and frustration have combined to beget future anarchy, apocalypse and, of course, scars.

There is an incongruous reference to Belafonte's song, "Scarlet Ribbons" in which a little girl prays for and miraculously receives a gift of scarlet ribbons from an unidentifiable source. In Questel's version the scarlet ribbons are "ribbons of / voices cut": meaning, perhaps, that the objective of detaining people on Nelson Island was to cut their throat of dissent, to assassinate conversation as Martin Carter, talking about the murder of Walter Rodney in Guyana, put it nearly a decade later. Questel, foreshadowing his senior poet, recognizes detention and exile on Nelson Island as a purblind, one-eyed, Cyclopean strategy to cut the throat of the voice. The State, he fears has succeeded only too well; but the State may in the process have birthed a future of ineradicable scars in a botched Caesarian delivery.

(6)
"Hic Jacet"

In "Hic Jacet," an end-poem whose title is the same as Walcott's "Hic Jacet,"[25] "jacet" becomes 'jacket' owing to an error made by the "printer's devil". This jacket then covers the entire collection.

> the isolated
> fiction of commitment
> which burns to its own truth,

In Questel's vision, art proceeds from the isolated mind of the poet. It is fiction, yet it is also "its own truth". This suggests that for Questel at this juncture in his rapid evolution, the truth of a poem's fiction did not extend beyond the poem. The poem is, and demands commitment that is not political, ideological or even moral, to its own intense truth. "Truth" emerges only through a process of burning. One recalls the image in "Pan Drama" of the Pan Maker burning and hammering the steel in order to tune the instrument. But this burning and hammering, the pain and stuff of process, is not itself "truth", but only the severe pathway towards truth. The "fiction of commitment" burns *to* not *with* its own truth.

"Hic Jacet" begins, "As the Word / falls with ancient trees", a reference to the collapse of Questel's faith in religion and Adam's Fall from Eden, which resulted in the Fall of Nature and all things that Adam had named. Falling out of faith, Questel must now subsist without the foundation of a rooted belief. "Hic Jacet" ends with a sort of affirmation:

> as here
> spare flesh points

a situation knotted

to the bone

rooted

What is affirmed here is a tremulously rediscovered faith of the fallen human mind, whose untrustworthy Muse is now the Devil, that legendary controller of all things fallen, particularly words that he, a trickster, twists in order to deceive. Questel's book of poems is now enswaddled by a book-jacket designed by the will or error of the printer's devil.

Yet the poem and poet, reduced, spare-ribbed, skeletal and concatenated, confused, "knotted," is also "rooted", the poet is a kind of Second Adam, self-accommodated to his fallen landscape, rooted to earth and things human, even though he, like the ancestral Blakean trees at the beginning of the poem, is fallen.

(7)
"The Epileptic Boy of February"
In "The Epileptic Boy of February" Questel takes another retrospective look at the February Revolution, focusing on its leader, Geddes Granger, who is reduced in this caricature to "boy" and to Dostoevsky's Idiot, Prince Myshkin, a frothing prophet whose utterances are the result of uncontrollable seizures. Though Granger is located in a clearer context than most of Questel's protagonists, he is also presented as more symbol than realistic agent, and 1970 is portrayed as phenomenon and grand signifier.

The first observation is that Granger was indifferent to what would happen – the devastation of emotions and expectations – if he failed. Secondly, he lacked a coherent sense of both history and the slow, snail-like nature of how change occurs in history. Thirdly, he was drunk on his own rhetoric: "the rum/mage/ that is language." Fourthly, his vision was fixed on past ruins. He was

hungup on a
rack and
ruined rear-view-mirrored
vision of reality

Fifthly, his message, gut-bucket and rhythmic as traditional old-time Jazz, was also, more often than not, improvised.

Questel concludes that Granger's fate was that of the sacrificial and sacrificed prophet, Krishna / Christ, "lost in a seasonless land". He was one with the mad, the ecstatic, the dispossessed, the possessed, the sufferers, the poets:

> who bom
> bard
> the streets
> singing
> for their sanity

The breaking of "bombard" into "bom" and "bard" connects the Epileptic Boy to both the bums and the bards, the old-time balladeers, impoverished street singers, calypsonians, travelling minstrels, street-corner crossroads congregations of Shouter Baptists and poets.

This is Granger interiorized, transformed into symbol and mask for Questel's personal trauma

> [he] felt the pain of nothing
> numbing his mind
>
> numbering his days

Granger's encounter with "the pain of nothing" is Questel's encounter with the "blank" that he perceived both in society and within his mind. The Epileptic Boy enters a void, a region of soul-numbing tiredness and acedia which is more Questel's than Granger's.

> Now
> today
> somewhere in the corner of
> his skull
> a tiredness grows

This is Questel's description of mental exile, disconnection, residence in some indefinite region of the skull, "somewhere", an insecure retreat because it is subject to an indefinite but growing tiredness, a numbness of mind and a sense that his days are numbered: an intuition of death.

Questel, although he had neither marched nor allowed himself to be caught up in the snail's quantum leap from the security of a protective shell into the naked glare of the sunlight of 1970, and despite his developing aesthetic of hermeticism, did at a certain level, empathise with what was, after all, the most compelling public drama of his life time. His worrying question was: what happens to the catalysts whose passion, mania and soul-stirring rhetoric propel these short-lived movements towards apocalyptic anticlimax? He "identifies" with Granger to the extent that the latter's tiredness becomes "the worm in" "his own" "pea-green heart."

Questel learns to shape the rigid tension of the epileptic on the verge or in the throes of being possessed. Granger is a pilgrim making society's "stations, shango-shocked," and eventually arriving at his final cross: a state of exile more profound than the exile he once endured on Nelson Island: a state of alienation from a now silent, indifferent people, whose frenzy he had once both inspired and represented:

> somewhere in the corner of
> his skull
> your
> tiredness grows
>
> somewhere

The tiredness that the leader absorbs is no longer the indefinite "a" tiredness but "*your*" tiredness: both the tiredness of Questel, who schizophrenically had begun to address himself in the second person, and the collective tiredness of the people. The isolation is absolute because the leader's tiredness does not bend him or bind him closer to the people, but alienates him more profoundly from them, and them from him.

Questel would have savoured the irony of his final word in the "Epileptic Boy of February," the word "somewhere" which recalls the plaintive and yet triumphant ending of "There's a Place for Us", but differs from it in the profound tiredness and untriumphant bewilderment of Questel's protagonist. Numb of mind, weary of spirit, his message now is not one of hope. There is no Golden City on his horizon.

(8)

In "Wreck," the last of these 1972 poems, Questel offers the reader a synopsis of the roles he has played and the poses he has assumed throughout the twenty poems. He has been fool, "Jack of all spades", yet he has been independent in his thoughts: "mastered by none". He's been involved and detached, "steered between ole mas" – (that is the Jouvert Morning Carnival of the demi-monde that was the 1970 Revolution) and half-mast – (that is, the time of death and lamentation, the Ash Wednesday of the aftermath).

He has been "needled by rhetoric", pricked, initiated and drugged by the oratory of the revolution's demagogues. (There is no evidence in the poems that Questel ever succumbed to rhetoric; there is, rather, every sign that he resisted, mocked and condemned it. He was too much a sceptic to do otherwise). He has been "carded/for the threadmill." Here, with small elation he spins out this idea of needle, thread and card, the card being an iron instrument with teeth used "to part, comb out and set in order fibres of wool [or] hemp" (*Oxford Dictionary*). This image suggests that he felt that his existence was under the control of whoever was the Spinner of threads or the Weaver of fates. While he felt a constant impulse to rebel against such control, he generally emerged from such skirmishes with the Schemer of Things or Weaver of Threads or divine Pan Maker, tired and with a sense of entrapment. As product of the Caribbean plantation he recognizes life, work and history as having been a dance on the treadmill; that is, an arduous journeying on one spot, in which the traveller and travailler gets nowhere, despite the dangerous and potentially crippling ordeal of the dance.

Emerging from such situations and processes of being entrapped, controlled and worn out by the ordeal of a journey that cycles the traveller to nowhere, Questel's protagonist enters the vacuum at the storm's centre

> I follower
> flounder
>
> Sell
> my frenzy to the Trade Winds
> my beating
> memory to the doldrums

Here, he merges his identity with the now disillusioned followers of the leaders of the Black Power Revolution. He then renounces politics, love, religion; succumbs to pointless sexuality and finally drowns his loneliness in alcohol.

Hitting the bottle, my faith splinters.

This lovely wry-blue line captures precisely what happened to the revolutionaries. Some got drunk, others succumbed to narcotics of one kind or another – (the word "needled" signalled this destination) – most opted out. I didn't know of Questel as a drinker. I think the "wreck" he portrays here is more his generation than himself. No follower, he interweaves his personal narrative of failure, lost faith and motivation and his profound sense of anticlimax and emptiness, with that of the failed and foundered rebels of 1970.

III: NEAR MOURNING GROUND

On 24th July 1975, Victor Questel gave me a collection of fourteen poems which he called *Lines, Circles and Tracks*. In an Author's Note he explained that:

> Now that SCORE has been closely examined by Winston [i.e. Winston Hackett who wrote a review essay of SCORE entitled "Survival"[26]] I feel that the time is ripe for the coming together of the better poems written since 1972.

He promised that *Lines, Circles and Tracks* would "one day form part of a book of poems to be called ON MOURNING GROUND". The fourteen poems were "Cut", "Lines", "Words and Gestures", "Blindman's Bluff", "No Pain", "Near Mourning Ground", "Only Believe", "Amayirikiti", "The Joker", "For Real", "Man Dead", "Seagull", "Solutions" and "The Track." On 24th May, 1976 Questel produced another slim collection that consisted of "Triangles of Sound", "Grandad", "Dawn", "The Weather Eye", "Fire and Ash", "Father" and "View". Poems from the 1975 and 1976 collections were to form the body of *Near Mourning Ground* (1978)

Mourning Ground is a Spiritual Baptist rite of initiation into a deeper faith in which the 'mourner' after a period of fasting, prayer and trance is granted, if worthy, gifts by the Holy Spirit. During mourning seven seals or bandages prevent the pilgrim from looking outward on the world. These seals, by forcing the pilgrim to look only inwards facilitate possession by the Holy Spirit. In a few significant poems Questel sought access into the Spiritual Baptist experience of one section of his family as a possible guide to reconstructing his own foundation of belief, and moving out of the Doldrums in which, like the narrator of "Wreck" his spirit lay becalmed. Movement out of the Doldrums, however, was an ordeal in itself, as the opening poem "Sea Blast"[25] illustrates.

(1)
"Sea Blast"

"Sea Blast" is a meditation on the image of the *Federal Maple*, one of the two inter-island ferryboats that linked together the islands of the defunct West Indian Federation. The other was named *The Federal Palm*. A gift from the Canadian Government, these ships cost much to be maintained, and when the Federation itself ran aground a mere three years after its inauguration in January 1958, it seems that *The Federal Maple* was abandoned to the elements and ended up permanently moored in a dockyard.

Questel chose the rusting *Federal Maple* as his image of relentless deterioration. The ship's ageing captain tries to maintain his waning manhood amidst decline and downfall. A dry, hard unsentimental portrait of the nullification that Time brings, "Sea Blast" unmasks dead ideas, dead passion, pointlessness and decrepitude beneath the face of self-confidence. The captain can be any of the various "fathers" of the defunct Federation who were also the "fathers" of the newly independent island-nations, the anachronistic steersmen of rusting ships of state that are going nowhere. The captain of *The Federal Maple,* drunk and unmanned, still imagines himself at the helm of his foundering vessel and still "charts a course he will sail no more".

(2)
"Seagull"

"Sea Blast," like "Wreck", reveals a new Questel, whose narrative is rooted in a clear and definite context. The syntax is more relaxed, the line more expansive; though the eye is still relentless and the laughter as grey as before. "Seagull," the poem that succeeds "Sea Blast", is a type of poetic review of the Trinidad and Tobago Theatre Workshop's production of Chekhov's *The Seagull* in 1975. In that play the rural innocence of a young woman is destroyed when she falls in love with a cynical bored writer, Boris Trigorin, who visits her village and involves her in his dead, failed life. Curiously, a similar thing had been happening in the private lives of certain members of the Theatre Workshop. There was the developing relationship between Derek Walcott, the Company's playwright, and Norline Metevier, a young dancer who was given the main role of Nina, the young woman whose sanity is destroyed through her affair with Trigorin, an older man.

Albert Laveau, the Theatre Workshop's most versatile, and along with Errol Jones, most accomplished actor, returning to the "village" of Trinidad and Tobago after having failed to make an impression in the United States, played the part of the cynical visitor to the village. It was deadly. Laveau did not have to act. He was simply playing himself and his pain of disappointment which he masked with a pose of insouciance and indifference. Questel saw in Laveau the figure of Dedalus whose hubris took him on a flight "too close to the sun". Toppling back to the confining earth of the Caribbean village, Dedalus "fires one", that is, consoles himself with alcohol (rather like the disillusioned "pilgrims" after the collapse of the 1970 Revolution). There was ironic humour in this portrait. Questel knew that "Fire one" was the Devil's drunken and grimly comic toast after his plantation was set fire in *Ti Jean and His Brothers*, and that Laveau had registered a most memorable performance of the triple roles of Papa Bois, Planter and Devil in Walcott's 1970 production of that play.

Returned from "failure" in the United States, Laveau, typecast as Chekov's burnt-out writer Trigorin is

> bored as he looks at actors
> burning to be the actor he has become,
>
> but trapped in their roles.

The reader recognizes this as yet another Questel scenario of entrapment, struggle to break loose and failure: "the ash of effort" as he terms it elsewhere. What began as a meditation on the Theatre Workshop, that distinguished and iconic post-Independence macrocosm of the struggle in the wider society for world-class excellence, becomes a contemplation of Questel's personal effort to sever umbilical ties and to break free of fixed roles that life, fate, God, society – whoever or whatever is the artistic director of destinies – has imposed on him. He dearly wants to cut or loosen

> the knot that
> has tied you [i.e. himself] to the ribbed tree reaching
> for the sky

As usual, Questel's endeavour fails and he becomes neither free agent in his choice of role, nor actor playing whatever role the director assigns him, but a lifeless, static stage-prop.

> You are now
> the stuffed fish on the mantle piece
> caught by the gull
> like any actor
> reflecting with one weather eye
> that is not his,
> or of his sea-
> son

So the poem, beginning as a commentary on the Theatre Workshop's performance of *The Seagull*, is really about being fixed in roles that some director, external to one's will, assigns. The ending is dreadful; the fixity is one of death, the frozenness absolute and beyond escape.

(3)
"Lament"

"Lament" is a pun on Lamont. A relic from the period of the 1940s and 1950s, Lamont aspired to be a lawyer but may have failed; or he may have succeeded, then been defeated by a mental breakdown. The Caribbean with its limited opportunities for social ascent via the ladder of education and success at the professions of mainly law and medicine, was full of examples of those who failed. Lamont was one of those. Questel's portrait of his mild delusion, as well as his naming of the poem, "Lament", shows his empathy with this failed scholar, whose failure was symbolic of a deeper one: the region's failure to affirm an identity beyond the Afro-Saxonism of the old colonial system.

Lamont keeps only British time. He awaits the next Empire Day celebrations. So, in a sense, does his society which is caught in a cyclic movement back to the same colonialism he represents, more obviously and absurdly than they. So Lamont represents the overlapping of one age into another, of time past into time present. He is a symbol, not only of what

211

the Caribbean has left behind, but of what it is taking forward into the future. He should be read alongside the apparently so different captain of the rusting *Federal Maple*. The one genteel, neatly attired in dark legal suits, cultured and polite, the other dishevelled, gross, self-deluded: decadent together they represent the nation's and, the region's failure. They are what the region has inherited and must redeem: its derelict personhood.

(4)
"View" and "The Weather Eye"

"View" is set in Santa Margarita, the hill above the town of St. Augustine, where a substantial portion of the earlier archives of Derek Walcott used to be housed at the home of one of the University's librarians, a close friend of Walcott's. Questel, who was doing research for his PhD on Walcott, was tracking down an unpublished early play, *Harry Dernier* or *Harry the Last*. The poem provides us with his impressions of the librarian, a wonderfully kind and gracious lady who, like Lamont, represents an entire era, fading away. Not long after Questel's visit, she suffered a nervous breakdown.

> She gently goes mad on my mind
> hooked to the blue
> caught in the tail-spin
> of these collapsing times

Questel used the first line of this quotation – the name of a then popular song, "Gentle on My Mind"[28] – in the early poem, "Sister". It is this "madness" invading the serenity and gentility of Afro-Saxon civilization that is Questel's subject here. Madness is the boy flying the kite of his aspirations and fantasies somewhere in the hills, then feeling the thread in his hand go limp as the kite, no longer under his control, "drifts through the smoke / towards the sea." Questel, adrift himself, identifies with both the boy and the kite, and of course, with his hostess, whose thread seems also to have snapped. He ends with his usual jesting wry humour:

> Santa Margarita, pray for us
> deliver us from our many accents and stresses
> too acute for our minds

"The Weather Eye", for Leroy Clarke, signals the arrival or return of Leroy Clarke, painter and pointer, creator of a portfolio of pen drawings, and poet on a mission. Questel's poem is an impressionistic review of Clarke's drawings and poetry. Its central concern, however, is Questel's awareness of his own inner tensions and his sense of helplessness in the grip of incipient mental collapse. As in "Seagull", he sees himself as a lifeless prop on life's absurd stage, where all motion is cyclic and repetitive. He is "a stuffed fish / on tenter hooks".

> as I turning with the recorder's spool
> run
> myself down
> while longing for the stillness
> of its centre

Clarke, like Questel, is a native of the peri-urban village of Gonzalez, and Questel is attracted to Clarke's energy, powerful self-mythologization and "the blind fury" of his use of language.

> as a double axe
> to split the myths that have fenced us in

This portrayal of Clarke as an avatar of Shango recognizes Clarke's fury as a force directed towards either a blind destruction of ancestral myths or a violent opening up of these myths; in the fences that society has long been hemmed in by. Questel, helping here to create the Clarke myth, heralds his presence and invites other loa: Anansi, Brathwaite's world-maker, word-breaker and creator, and snail, Walcott's hermetic, self-contained, solipsistic spirit-guide, to look out for and take note of Clarke's explosive presence.

(5)
"Fire and Ash", "Coconut", "No Pain".
Clarke's advent opens up new possibilities, but can Questel access them? "Fire and Ash", the very next poem, suggests, "No". The image of burnt canes with which "Fire and Ash" begins is prominent in Brathwaite's *Islands,* though common enough among other Caribbean writers. In Questel, burnt cane is an image of history that has become "burnt out", "unburied", "unsung", but miraculously still alive. It is also related to the harmattan, "each new season / that brings dust", as in Brathwaite's *Harmattan Poems* (1971) such as "Sun Song" that Questel had read by the mid-1970s.

The cane image is tenuously sustained in the image of a policeman directing traffic with hands like windmills "grinding this morning's traffic/ to a halt". The policeman becomes an automation, slave to the wound up "wheel of law", and capable of mastering only "elementary rules / like 'Stop'." The policeman thus becomes yet another version of man as trapped and reduced object, deprived of will and under control of whoever winds up his springs. His windmills of arms signify the burnt-out, mind-dead, zombified protagonist – Questel himself at that point of intersection – where the bright cane fire of affirmation becomes the white-grey ashen barrenness of negation.

> For a moment he circles his mind's black out.
> He is now a frightened animal
> caught in a headlamp's flame

He also sees his condition in the streetwalker, a woman reduced to

> the loose piece of flesh
> that
> paces the pavement
>
> beating out its sole track
> on the corner

This figure appears on Questel's landscape during moments of stress, but sex, as always, is no escape. Masturbation, an alternative to sex, is both release and ordeal. The sequestered protagonist "turns his hands once more, grinding." The turning hands, the grinding, fuse the images of sugar-mill and robot.

> so like the ridden down trodden
> mule he is
> he kicks at history's stable door
> and
> turns his hands once more
>
> grinding

A sterile beast of burden, his rebellion against his situation has become a futile gesture, a kicking against "the stable door" of history, where stable also means firm, unyielding, safely locked. Like the traffic police-man's, his hands become windmills and he an automaton. Poet, peasant, policeman, streetwalker are all part of the meaningless grind and revolution of the sugar mill.

(6)
"Coconut"

What Questel sees when he "circles his mind's black-out", is a cracking-up of its protective shell. "Coconut" is about this cracking-up; its suddenness, its violence, its irreparable destruction of the psyche and the privacy of its pain. Mental seizure or attack is a violent process in which the sufferer, in the grip of some uncontrollable force, is shattered, as one cracks a coconut with its three eyes, by smashing it on stone. This is the cruellest and most painful statement in Questel's poetry of the alienated vision in an opaque, blank universe of stone. The poem is packed with instances of pain. Even the donkey pulling the vendor's cart is whipped on the nose. The nails of the woman peeling the coconut branch are broken, the shell likewise. The broken pieces of *skull*[29] are unceremoniously swept and thrown into the garbage bin. The loneliness is absolute, so no one knows, not even those who are a stone's throw away, that this has been happening.

Yet Questel suggests that the cracking of the skull and the bruising of the eye are necessary for new vision to emerge. The water that pours out of the dry nut is, symbolically, stale. It is no longer the nourishing and palatable water of the old vision or faith. After this "sudden-time of the lost mind/ in your head / that is cracked", the image changes to that of the water-coconut vendor in his donkey cart returning home with his cargo of split shells. The focus is on his dogged and certain journey home after a day or night of chopping and splitting open nuts. This figure had appeared before in Derek Walcott's "Nights in the Garden of Port of Spain"[30] where:

> As daylight breaks the Indian turns his tumbril
> of hacked, beheaded coconuts towards home

There, so soon after Independence, Walcott had intuited the potential of the city to erupt suddenly in a revolution of the Third Estate that just might be directed, as in the French Revolution, towards the aristocrats of the ancient regime. (Or perhaps not; any such revolution in multi-ethnic Trinidad and Tobago would more likely pit the ethnically divided proletariat in a violent confrontation of the two major races – as had happened in the mid-sixties in British Guiana – soon to be renamed Guyana – next door).

Questel's employment of the donkey cart / peasant image first appeared in "Linkages" where:

> The donkey cart moves forward
> with
> the slowness of indentured peoples
> with the ease born of certainties
> I
> shall never feel
>
> its rounded syllables
> of movement
> mocking
> my liquid style

There the assumption seemed to be that the formerly indentured Indian traveller was more culturally secure, or less violated, undermined or erased than his Afro-Trinidadian counterpart. One notes, however, that the peasant's journey in "Linkages" is not towards what is today being termed the "homeland" south of the Caroni River, but north towards the city, where all pastoral pilgrims, rooted and certain or rootless and lacking in direction, are headed for the museum and entombment.

In "Coconut", the focus is on the vendor's dogged and certain journey home, which suggests to the poet that he too has, like his Panman Muse in "Pan Drama", to "push on" in spite of the fragmentation and emptiness that have possessed him. Nowhere in Questel is this quest for wholeness and coherence sentimental or predictable, nor is any refuge sought in conventional notions of artist as one who reconciles the splintered fragments of experience. The woman who makes a broom from the coconut palm and sweeps out the fragments of broken shell is not wife but Muse. The act of sweeping, so reminiscent of Afro-Caribbean and older West African funeral and sanctification rites, is a ritual act of purgation in which the spirit of the dead person or past is dismissed, is laid to rest, and the dwelling-place purged so that the living might reconcile themselves, both to the fact of death and the necessity of their own continued existence.

Questel's Muse, then, does not restore what has been shattered. She instead prepares the house of the psyche for the task of pushing on, by sweeping it clean of the ruins of the past. But she is a thoroughly Trinidadian Muse, who cleanses her own house then dumps the garbage on the road. So the fragments of shell are revealed to "the dazzling ray of sun/stroke" in a mesmerizing transition from darkness to light. Emerging from one's turbulent and pain-filled inner world, one may be blinded by the glare of the exterior universe. The function of Questel's Muse reverses the conventional myth in which a Spirit-guide or Sybil enables the poet's descent into a dark underworld: – the Id, the Inferno, the Unconscious, the dream-domain of the dead and not yet reincarnated ancestors.[31] Questel's Muse has a different task: that of facilitating an ascent or return to surface light where the poet's anxiety is made public even as he transcends the actual occasion of his mind's splintering. This process of ascent and return is a delicate one, bearing its own pain; so the poet retains a certain mystery and distance. He keeps himself.

> a stone's throw away
from everyone
so no one is clear about the broken pieces of skull
in that dazzling ray of sun
stroke

(7)

"*No Pain*"

It may seem harshly ironic that "Coconut", a poem about pain and trauma, should be followed by one entitled "No Pain", but for the fact that "No Pain" is a terse commentary on one of the most painful novels in the Caribbean canon, Harold Sonny Ladoo's *No Pain Like This Body*, a story about disintegration, alcoholism, madness, a family's naked exposure to swamp, snake, scorpion, mud, monsoon and near absorption into an almost primordial landscape. Ladoo's novel shatters the illusion that the journey of the ex-indentured Indian peasant has been any less grim or any more certain than that of the rest of Trinidad society. In 1975, the only equal to *No Pain Like This Body* was Harris's *The Far Journey of Oudin*, a similar anatomy of the "breaking-up and making-up"[32] of a community's world-view, culture, language and sense of the holy. The pundit, his congregation, the Gods and the rituals through which the community seeks to retain contact with them are all degraded. "The holy man farts during the wake's rituals."

Questel recognizes his own irreverence in the young boy's dismissal of God as "playing the ass", and appreciates the gross down-to-earth humour of the community as mask and mechanism of survival in face of continuous defilement and loss. The community of Tola Trace is trapped at the threshold of the New World where Legba, the former Dahomean Sun-God, now manifests as an old, crippled, one-legged hunchback who, however, still rules the crossroads of choice and beginning, while the East Indian deities experience a parallel mutation as they cross the Dark Water of their Middle Passage. This state of mutual diminishment is recognized by Questel as offering a slight possibility for the still querulous "African" and "Indian" communities to acknowledge a common ground and predicament on which they will, perhaps, build.

As a mind stripped of ritual and disconnected from all ancestral Gods, he addresses Legba with blasphemous irreverence, as if Legba were indeed no more than a one-legged cripple and not the Muse and Avatar of all new setting forth.

> What you say
> one
> foot
> as at the gate of cultures
> Nanny raining blows
> on the drum
>
> and crossing water

Legba and Nanny, grandfather and grandmother figures represent different versions of the same possibility. Nanny, the grandmother, beats a persistent drum in the ears of Gods that have ceased to listen. She represents the will and faith to reconnect and is the single image of hope to emerge from *No Pain Like This Body*. Legba, like Nanny, signifies the diminished, distorted past, and yet remains crucial to new beginning. Questel's query, unanswered in the poem as it still is in the society, is whether Legba recognizes the significance of Nanny and the drum beat to which she clings. It could, of course, be posed the opposite way: Does Nanny acknowledge and understand the significance of Legba? Question for the bards.

(8)

"Words and Gestures"

Completed in July 1975 and announced as part of a collection of fourteen poems that Questel thought represented "the better poems written since 1972", "Words and Gestures" first appeared in February 1973 as "Letter to My Brother". That absent brother may be the "you" addressed in the poem's first lines:

> I can never quite imagine you behind glass
> though that is where I think you are now

Glass is a signifier of separation, relative or absolute. It could be, for example, the glass of a coffin or simply that of a windowpane. The parent poem of "Words and Gestures" may be Derek Walcott's "A Village Life"[33] where glass is an image of the distance of memory through which Walcott now perceives his deceased friend.

"Words and Gestures" begins with the voice of a narrator who is desperately isolated from and longs to be acknowledged by an absent Other.

> Smash your pane or
> I'll burn out slowly between the lines
>
> empty as an unshaded sketch

We are on familiar ground: the protagonist as cartoon figure trapped within the frame of the lines and facing burnout, blackout and break-down. Here, he confesses his need for communication and embrace that he will not get, since the Other, the "you" whom he addresses seems either to have killed himself or attempted suicide in a game of Russian roulette. For, how else can one read the lines:

> shattered by the shot
> blank
> in your brain?

Section II sustains the situation of gazing at things through glass. The narrator describes a snail creeping towards undergrowth; a slow process that is observed through his "windowed stare" – perhaps his lenses. He loses focus as the snail enters the bush

> and colour

219

> runs along the darkening brain
> dripping shapes to the glare of
> half-blind eyes

Literally, the external image disappears and the whole picture blurs because he is crying or because raindrops or liquid of some sort smears his lenses; or because, having removed his spectacles, he becomes "half-blind." Reading more deeply, the blurring of the external image points to an interior state, a condition of mind. The blurred lens the colour of maybe, blood, running "along the darkening brain" is connected with the idea in the previous section of a bullet, real or imagined, shot into the brain.

What does Questel make of or mean by these real or imaginary images, omens or sign posts? He provides a hint through the cryptic conclusion of Section II.

> Possessed
> all I own
> are my scribal impulses
>
> learning like any snail
> that
> home is where I'm locked in.

The snail becomes a complex image of entrapment, both in the domestic ménage of a place called home, and in the prison of the inner self. Both of these traps seem to be under the control of some jailer over whom the narrator has no control. The snail is also an image of the isolated, hermetic poet, concerned ultimately with narcissistic inner processes, though these may well be triggered or inspired by a perception of exterior phenomena.

Carnival, society's most elaborate and varied spectacle becomes the subject of the next section (Section III). When viewed through Questel's blurred lenses Carnival becomes transformed into:

(i) the season of national dust, heat, bronchitis and influenza

(ii) the season when the communal, penetrating sound of steelbands mocks the lonely interior voice of the guitar

(iii) the season that stretches between Christmas (the crib) and Lent/Good Friday (the Cross). Carnival is when

> masqueraders like their God

shuffle between the crib
and the cross
crabbing their stations to
prizes

"Words and Gestures" was originally finished in February 1973, during the Carnival season when Lord Kitchener sang "Rainorama", a calypso that immortalized the previous year's historic Carnival of May 1972. The traditional Carnival had been postponed from February to the rainy month of May ostensibly because of a polio outbreak earlier in the year. Polio, which cripples the young, becomes for Questel a symbol of the crippledom of a nation of masqueraders, whose dance becomes reduced to a shuffle then to a crab-like crawl. The crab image popular in West Indian writing of the 1960s[34] is in "Words and Gestures" an extension of the snail image. At the surface level it refers to the masqueraders' and, by extension, the nation's uncertain zig-zig movement towards rewards that are not only illusory, but cruelly disappointing.

The "stations" are points along the Carnival route where the masquerade is judged. They are also police stations in which steelband riot or political demonstration (another form of masquerade) ends. The stations are finally, stations of the cross, visible along several hillsides throughout Trinidad (for example, San Juan, St. Joseph, Mt. St. Benedict etc.). Questel's reading of Carnival from his own alienated snail-like or crab-like hermetic isolation, is deconstructive in the extreme. He perceives that not only Roman Catholic Trinidad, but the Creator God himself is caught up in a *via dolorosa* that begins with Carnival's swaggering, drunken crab-dance, and ends in stumble and stagger towards imprisonment (note the recurrence of the 'trap' image) and ultimately, crucifixion.

The crab image suggests an even more complex one: that of the sea shell:

the ocean's roars of their life-blood
sucked into the sunken shells of drums

Here is a wonderful compression of ideas that illustrates Questel's growth as a poet since his first collection. The ocean here is the Atlantic. Questel agrees with fellow-poet Malik ("Pan Run II") that "mih blood never stop running cross mih middle passage" and accepts Malik's affirmation that the urban experience has not destroyed the primal music which is reborn of the ocean.[35] He would also agree with both Malik and Dr. J.D. Elder[36] that the steelband is the latest re-creation of the ancestral African drum in the New World. In this respect, crossing the Middle Passage resulted in the channelling of the original music into other "shells" – "the sunken shells of drums."

The idea of continuity is strengthened by the word "sunken" which could mean lying deep in the waters of the unconscious. Haitian mythology has depicted the Atlantic Ocean as the home of the first ancestors, the Guinea dead, who became the first souls to be acknowledged in ceremonies of remembrance. Brathwaite would write of "the deep/sleeping sound of the bay",[37] a region of consciousness that counterbalanced the empty roads, broken claypots, govis and ruins of the New World diasporan. Walcott would later sum it up in his poem, "The Sea Is History"[38]. Questel, whose vision in "Words and Gestures" is of both "timber", solid seasoned wood of ancestral heritage, and "termites," invisible and indefatigable agencies of erosion, qualifies the emerging myth of the Atlantic as a still potent vault of undead memory and psychic energy. So the image of "shells of drums" works in the opposite direction to suggest that what now remains of original African consciousness is only an empty husk.

"Shell" is also a reference to the conch shell of the plantation that summoned the enslaved to work or sometimes to rebellion. It certainly is an allusion to the extension of imperialism built on slave labour into the parasitism of today's multinational corporations such as Shell and Texaco, which exploit ("suck") Trinidad's and the world's petroleum resources. The "sunken shells of drums" are, in fact, both the empty discarded oil drums of a now distant past, which the exploited people sink, etch and tune to create their music – (at times under the sponsorship of the very vampires – e.g. Shell Invaders or BP Renegades – and the oil drums into which the country's economic life blood is sucked for an export that is far less profitable to the country than it should be.

Questel is writing here with the density of image and complexity of wordplay and allusion characteristic of the Brathwaite of *Islands*, from whom he has obviously learned much. The "trap" that he reveals here is simultaneously a cultural, economic and existential one in which the masqueraders, hypnotised, shuffle and crawl

their life-style
caught in the glass eyes of cameras

"Caught" is both photographed and trapped. The fact that the cameras have glass eyes is an indication of the blind indifference of the spectators for whom the masquerade is being performed – soucouyants on holiday. In *Invisible Man*, Ralph Ellison employs glass and glass eyes as images of either the distorted vision of stereotyping whites, or of such blacks as have accepted their invisibility. Similarly, Brathwaite's Puritan/capitalist god and empire-builder Jah, lives in a world of glass. So do Jah's humble servants, who are reduced to the role of trapped goldfish and perpetual open-mouthed performers swimming in circles. Questel's employment of the glass image suggests that the Caribbean man is also at one and the same time creator and minstrel, musician and dancing clown, sharing with his Afro-American counterpart Jah's extended prison of glass. There is also an allusion to the old native superstition that to be photographed is to lose one's soul to spirit thieves.

If some of what has gone before suggests a mind that has responded sensitively and critically to Brathwaite's seminal work, some of what follows indicates Questel's thorough familiarity with Walcott's poems and plays. The lines:

lost in this folk-
mass
my cleft brain
paces Papa Bois's
heel

are clearly a response to poems such as Walcott's "Mass Man" and "Junta"[39] and the 1958 play, *Ti Jean and His Brothers*, which Walcott revised and rewrote in 1970.[40] There is the sense of schizophrenia ("my cleft brain") powerful in Walcott's *The Castaway and other Poems* and in some of his *Trinidad Guardian* articles of the sixties.

"Folk mass" has three meanings: "crowd of folk", "folk masquerade" and the mod-type religious services with which the Roman Catholic Church had begun to experiment in the wake of the Black Power intrusion into their cathedral in 1970 and the steady expansion of fundamentalist sects that began during the same period. Spokesmen for reform in the traditional Christian community – Roman Catholic,

Anglican, Presbyterian – advocated the localization of the liturgy and Church music. There also began to be Calypso competitions in Roman Catholic schools which, two decades earlier, might have been sending their children on special retreat to pray for the souls of those who would be enjoying the revelry of Carnival. The Eucharist and the Passion were choreographed in a few churches after 1970.

Many view "folk mass" as another form of "ole mas" and Questel, sceptical about most things, becomes Walcott's Mi-Jean, a paralysed pseudo-intellectual contemplating the cloven hoof of the Devil, who is planter, politician, priest and the whole abstract intellectualism of the West that has helped produce so many sceptics in Europe and schizo-phrenics in the Caribbean. Questel therefore questions the capacity of Caribbean man to confront the Devil with Ti-Jean's innocence, wonder and mother-wit. Such qualities, he feels, are not recoverable, the way lost being the way lost. He thus succumbs to the futility of things, citing the chorus of a now defunct Road March, Sparrow's "Mas in Brooklyn" – "Play mas in yer mas" – and joins society in its minstrel shuffle.

> like the
> rest
> marred by my own make-
> believe.

Thus Questel the maker who, like the Walcott of "Mass Man", tries to establish his distance from the masquerade, realizes that in an age of unbelief and spiritual paralysis, the poet's isolated quest for truth may itself be a harmful substitution of mask for face and of style for verity. As agnostic, he believes only in what he has created. But what he has created is imperfect, the damaged product of his cleft brain and thus no basis for any belief. The separation of "make" from "believe" is a clear hint that the poet's "make-believe" is the imperfectly fabricated fiction of his poetry, in which he tries to make himself believe as he seeks a substitute for lost faith.

In Section Four, the poet, like Martin Carter in "Not Hands Like Mine", contemplates "the people's slow/strangulation", seeking an image or creed capable of releasing him from his vision of death. He does not find it. His quest leads him deeper into the shadow-land. His "uncertainty / finds substance in shadows, / even in the shadow of / life." This is his city of dreadful night which he entered when in "Fire and Ash" he began to circle his "mind's black-out". He continues to write, but doggedly, without elation, with self-contempt and without anything to say.

> my insanity
> out stares
> my reflexion

This means that all his thoughts are overwhelmed, his entire vision dominated by his madness. There is a conventional image of the protagonist staring at his reflection in a mirror, looking not through, but into glass, and turning his insane eyes away from his equally insane double, his *semblable* and brother who, as in Amos Tutuola[41] resembles him too much.

No reconciliation is achieved between exterior and interior worlds, between face and image, self and (br)other. Instead, the skeletal bill-boards of "Prelude" recur and

> even Nothing
> now trapped
> between skeletal bill-boards
> has lost its profundity.

If before Questel's sensibility had famished itself on existentialist philosophy of the Void, he now grows tired of such unsubstantial diet. "Nothing" has become a normal state, part of the all-pervasive ennui of things. The bill-boards suggest, as before, the collapse of the world of commoditization and advertisement. But they are also indicative of the protagonist's inner emptiness. He, like his society, has nothing to advertise, no self to flaunt and maybe nothing to write about.

Turning his gaze once more towards the common folk whom he had formerly presented as mere masqueraders, he can now perceive in them richer, more positive and wholesome ways of confronting death and void. The bongo dance, performed at wakes, used to be a way of celebrating the soul's passage from one plane of existence, life, to another, death. It is a symbol of the sort of reconciliation the poet seeks – the unification or atonement of the city-bred sensibility with the rural Afro-Caribbean cosmogony; the marriage of the isolated threadbare intellect to community, dance and the life of instinct.

But to grow tired of saying "No" is not the same thing as to regain faith, to say an affirmative "Yes". The journey back from the deadly Void of cerebration is hard for the city-bred Caribbean intellectual, though both poles are possible in his society, some of whose citizens drift schizophrenically between one and the other. For Questel

> the search lurches tiredly
> link my first
> embarrassed
> bongo
> step

Thus ends Section IV with a teetering gesture towards beginning. Section V begins with a corresponding "loss of balance" in his use of words:

> my loss of balance
>
> my slow grasp of words
> green in their insanity

The poem is slowly born out of all the foregoing pain and turmoil; but it is born inchoate. The poet contrasts his stumble into voice with the regular mechanical movement of the "iron mules in the oilfields". Technological man, the man of the future, however sterile ("mule") his work may appear to the poet, is certain of his truths and satisfied with their robot-like rigidity. The multinational corporations need no other poetry than the steady rhythm and sucking of those pumps and the mulish sweat of the exploited natives. The "green" poet, however, must face the insane chaos of the world inside and recover for the page words which appear jaundiced even as they become visible.

Love, that conventional ointment for all imaginable maladies of heart, mind or spirit, simply cannot survive in this atmosphere. Sex, too, becomes part of the general absurdity. The poet as lover or seeker of flesh, shrivels into Ralph Kripalsingh or some emptier cartoon figure:

> rasping with laughter
> as
> the comic artist encircles me
> in his lines
>
> while

> voices of mockery
> creep beneath my skull

The result of this attempt to communicate through death-dance, words and touch will be further retreat into the skull's closed circle and the adoption of a self-defensive mockery of his entrapment in the lines of the "comic artist," that Eshu-like, sinister and grinning god-figure.

Section VI begins with the word "poised" which may suggest a control of circumstances and a balance until one reads further.

> Poised
> like a painted
> Adam
> frozen
> between flight
> and the sting of revenge
> the dual attitude of both
> slave and citizen

It is not poise but fixity, a frozenness that the protagonist is confessing to here. The myths of Adam and Crusoe had been current in the writings of Derek Walcott since 1965. According to Walcott, the Caribbean and American peoples are, like Crusoe, inheritors of a New World which, like Adam, they have been accorded the sovereign privilege of naming. As Walcott knew, his privileged "inheritors" could more correctly be termed newcomers, intruders, involved not in "naming" but "renaming" terrain previously lived-in by the now decimated, marginalized, silenced and all but genocidally extinguished native Caribbean and American peoples. Questel, like Walcott, is aware of the presence of the Serpent in this paradise of imperfection. He therefore views the New World Adam as another fiction, one that is "eternal" because it is dead, frozen, unnatural and artificial.

The "painted Adam" image was derived from Walcott's use, in *In a Fine Castle*, of a painting by Watteau depicting a group of Caucasian settlers fleeing a tropical island. Some of them, though, keep looking backward nostalgically, even as their feet are on the gangplank of the ship. This shows that they are bound to the land they are trying to escape from. A similar conclusion also appears in Walcott's discourse on his adoption of Crusoe as the central metaphor of *The Castaway*.[42] There he notes the significance of the moment when Crusoe attempts to flee his island but cannot, since he realizes that he is now the only truly indigenized occupant of his "happy desert".

Crusoe's frozenness, like that of Watteau's refugees, suggests a confusion concerning identity. These Caucasians are Creoles for whom the island has been home, even though Europe is supposed to be the superior civilization of their ancestors. They are deeply divided now that the hated Afro-Creole underclass have begun to claim their right to rulership and – so white people of the immediate post-Emancipation and mid-twentieth century post-Independence periods have feared – to seek revenge on their erstwhile (and current) captors, owners, tormentors and sagacious patrons. The typical Derek Walcott play of the 1970s – *Dream on Monkey Mountain, In a Fine Castle, Pantomime* – seeks to explore the "terrified consciousness" of white Creoles, "mulattos" and blacks now that Prospero / Crusoe and Caliban / Friday have *apparently* reversed roles. *Pantomime* in particular ruminates on how Independence has affected the pantomime or masquerade of social relations on the island. Walcott has preached that the so-called "Afro-Saxon" and "mulatto" dilemmas are little different from the Euro-Creole dilemma – give a fine castle, take a fine castle, of course.

Questel recognizes the race/class quarrel in his tangled society as being another of history's traps. He speaks of himself as being frozen in "the dual attitude of both/ slave and citizen," though clearly, he was not alone in this dilemma. As Mannoni, Fanon and Memmi[43] were debating, this was *the* post-colonial problem *par excellence*. The "slave" (or "enslaved" as it has become more politically correct to say) doesn't cease to manifest the complex of attitudes inherited from enslavement, merely because Emancipation has been declared. The deep structures of the earlier period remain embedded in his/her psyche. Slave becomes "citizen", a privilege formerly confined to the proprietorial master class. Yet there is no clear transition from one pole of being to the other; only, instead, an unsteady, uncertain, tremulous oscillation, or, as Questel affirms, a sort of frozenness that is more terrifying than oscillation, since oscillation involves back and forth movement, while frozenness is death-in-life fixity.

In the second half of segment (VI), the poet's eye shifts focus once more to the world outside of him. He watches someone that he terms "you" "make another conquest". This "you" is different from the "you"

228

in Section (I) who seems to be a person with whom the narrator has lost contact and with whom he is seeking desperately to communicate. The "you" of Section (VI) is a conquistador who has taken advantage of the self-consciousness and insecurity of the pubescent nation, a predator (slave or citizen?) who has ravaged its/her innocence and naivete. The narrator, however, speaking out of his situation of frozenness and ambivalence promises

> I'll tell no one
> for the whispered word now
> could be the microphoned betrayal
> then

Self-exiled from the ethos of politics and clandestine predation, the narrator confesses his fear of that world and his equal fear of his society which would sooner betray the whistle-blower than confront the predator. The protagonist knows of the cowardice of his fellow-citizens even as he confesses his own, and makes his pragmatic choice not to become anyone's scapegoat in the post-1970 police state of secret evidence-gathering tribunals, where anyone could become an inform-ant, the self-protective, disconnected stance of the turtle or snail – the stance that Brathwaite in "4th Traveller"[44] later describes as "i-sol-ence" – was one of the stances many (if not most) people adopted. They kept themselves away from the dreadful power-play. This strategy which had been prevalent among the enslaved, later became part of the survivalist mechanism of colonial society as a whole. Questel's protagonist, frozen in "the dual attitude of both slave and citizen" is, whether slave or citizen, ultimately a trickster, sagacious, aware, but irresponsible to anyone or anything except his own survival. He is your old and new Caribbean man, whose emergence as "citizen" is stymied by his hidden identity as enslaved consciousness.

In Section VII the narrator addresses another "you", a female presence who had appeared from time to time in earlier poems as a shadow, perhaps a "dark lady". She is sometimes portrayed as devout, even nun-like. At others she is the reluctant target of his lust. Here, the narrator tries to convince her and himself that he is more than a painted, frozen, self-centred narcissist. He can also be batonnier. He must show that he is both stickman and snail, both nimble-footed dancer, warrior and champion of the public gayelle, and lonely isolato bound on a journey that is slow and private. Stickman and snail, he seeks to marry extroversion with introspection, the public with the private; the loneliness that like the chantwell's reaches out to chorus and community, with the loneliness which reaches inward to hermetic silence.

If he could only discover the stickman within himself he would also be able to release the stickman's self-assertive, heroic, hyperbolic rhetoric and conquer his reluctant not yet lover with language. With language alone? One asks. What does the poet's violent boastful address to this woman signify? Maybe he is pretending to be who he is not. He realizes that "walking / a straight line", the skill of the snail, "is not the same /as keeping your balance", the art of the stickman. He also is still trapped in what he earlier said was a circle drawn around him by the comic artist. He seeks a language that can break the circle or spell, but recognizes at last that:

> the circle is complete
> the violence is total
>
> It is the words
> that are mad
> the words

Whatever this ending means, Questel is talking in his own cryptic imagery about violent seizure and his loss of "balance", or control over words that issue of their own volition from his cleft brain. He may no longer be just snail – snails don't talk – but he is not yet stickman – stickmen talk, sing, and dance.

(9)
"Lines", *"Near Mourning Ground"*, *"Father"*
"Lines" for Robert Lee begins with six recurrent Questel images:

> *Frames cracked* by *lines*
> of doubt
> hold, the *cleft* note that is blown
> as you make that *journey across* this
> blank

Questel in considering the situation of a fellow poet, the likeable, well-balanced St. Lucian, Robert Lee, recognizes that Lee has been making a journey similar to the one he has been making, from youth to maturity and from the assurance of fixed traditional systems such as Christian faith, into empty, chaotic, blank or disorganized spaces outside of traditional systems. A *frame* such as Catholicism or Anglicanism or, for Questel, the still remote dreaded, censored spaces of the remnants of African belief systems – Orisha, Kélé in Trinidad and St. Lucia respectively – is now cracked by lines of doubt because of the European cultural imperialism that was central to the New World experiment. All the frames are cracked, yet Questel says that they "hold", that is, remain intact, or don't quite fall apart .

"Cracked" in its other connotation means schizophrenic, demented, divided. It was a keyword in the writings of both Walcott and Brathwaite whose dilemma was whether to view cracked systems as irretrievably ruined or whether the ensuing fragments might be viewed as broken off from something that was once whole, and capable of rebirth, regrowth, re-rooting and expansion in the New World of the Caribbean. Could healthy new cultures grow out of the haphazard remnants of older ancestral ones? This question, asked in various ways by Eric Williams [45] Derek Walcott and Kamau Brathwaite, was the great Afro-Saxon question at the time of Independence.

"Cracked" as "cleft note" is a sonic image: the cracked or cleft note of a jazz trumpet or saxophone. Horn players like Roland Kirk or Sonny Rollins were capable of producing two or three notes simultaneously, as if they were trying to make the schizoid consciousness audible in the sound of their horns. But Jazz was not only about alienation, splintering, loss of focus and madness as downhome folk consciousness encountered urban ghettos, which were the dark downside of modernization; Jazz, was also about reconciliation, self-healing and affirmation in spite of… So the cracked note isn't only an expression or recognition of schizophrenia, but an elated celebration of duality, of multiple selves and voices that have grown naturally out of a grim and unnatural history.

Questel observes Lee's "journey across this blank" – the wilderness or empty space outside of closed, safe systems. Journeying into the unknown demands the mapping of new space – as Columbus mapped all of his blind ventures into the Caribbean. Drawing the new maps, Questel argues, is more important than "simply journeying". But the new maps cannot be drawn without the "blind journeying". Their value is that they offer a possibility that future journeys need not be as blind.

Questel then points his silent acolyte, Lee, to what he might encounter in the wilderness: objects, half-remembered voices, unknown spirits, the need for but inadequacy of prayer or guidance. The first signposts in the wilderness are stone, a wet slate and the remembered childhood chant, prayer or spell: "Jumbie, Jumbie, dry mih slate." These signals are pointed out, with the caution that "it takes more than hope / to smash an image".

How should neophyte Lee read the signs foretold by his self-appointed mentor and predecessor? First there is "stone". The word stands stolidly at the beginning of the passage. Stone is barrier or boulder blocking the pilgrim's pathway, sealing the mouth of the cave, the *alta spelunca* into which all poets must descend to become acquainted with their own inner depths and darkness. Stone may also be a sign of the hardness or opacity that will confront the pilgrim on his journey into the wilderness

The slate invokes the related but unmentioned image of the frame. Slates used to have wooden frames to protect schoolchildren from their harsh edges. The usefulness of the slate in primary school education, was that it could easily be washed. Each old lesson was erased as the slate became again a grey, blank space ready for fresh cursive.

"Jumbie, Jumbie" – not yet the Haitian zombie, that product of the fantasizing Euro-American cinematic mind – the Jumbie was a ghost that the school child, lost in the wilderness of school, hoped would aid his/her passage through the chaos of words, sums, figures, lines and signs; the stones that were the dreaded hindrances in the life of the school child. The Jumbie, non-Christian, a creature of folklore usually relegated to the realm of superstition, was more trusted than the Trinity and/or the Saints who were normally on the side of the oppressors: teachers, priests, hierarchical sharers of licks.

Maybe the Jumbie was simply St. Paul's "Unknown God" who might possibly reinforce the efforts of the better known throngs of beneficent angels and saints. Both schoolboy and neophyte poet need the Jumbie, particularly the poet who chooses as his mission the smashing of images, the beating back of the "retreating rituals" of the system he is trying to discard. This system, despite his efforts, still retains power to affect and enframe what and how he sees. The small hope provided by the Jumbie relieves the seeker somewhat of his "growing tiredness".

Having, as he believes, passed through this first phase of the wilderness,

Questel feels entitled to advise his younger brother in life's school, that "Articles of faith are not enough". The Anglican "articles of faith" were meant to clarify the reasons for the breakaway of the rebellious Church of England from its ancestor, the Roman Catholic Church. Finding itself in a sort of theological wilderness, the Anglican Church codified its differences from its ancestor religion, in much the same way as Questel is trying to locate himself in new space after rebelling against a confining Anglicanism. He, however, recognizes that to substitute one coded system for another is to return to the same prison that one has been trying to escape. "Articles" belong to the already abandoned system and will not suffice for the poet's continuing encounter with the blank, the empty unknown.

There are temptations to be endured. One of these is the temptation to abandon the quest and circle back to a "cave" of refuge. The pilgrim poet must press on through "pure mist", "as you follow the tracks cut/yet/ tracing new lines". The second temptation is that of arrogance and hubris. There are such predecessors as bois-men (stick fighters noted for their supreme arrogance); hawks (cf Eric Roach's magnificent and doomed frigate-bird) and Jumbie birds (small night owls whose mournful cry is thought to signal death). The questing poet needs to be cautious of following such Muses. Aiming for the skies is one thing: trying to become a sun-god is another. All the myths warn against such hubris. There is the legend of Phaeton, Son of Apollo, who drove his father's chariot too close to Earth, and was struck down by a thunder bolt or lightning bolt sent by Zeus. There is the story of Dedalus who flew too close to the sun and perished when the wax holding together the feathers in his wings melted. There is the carrion crow in Wordsworth McAndrew's "Legend of the Carrion Crow" who, seeking to know what lay beyond the sky's limit, broke that barrier but burned to black cinder in doing so and was further condemned to perform the ordeal of scavenger consuming dead flesh.

Thus Questel, forewarned by such archetypes of the fallen aspirant to godhead, sees danger when "Your head is gathered in cloud" until it "becomes the sun"; one must "be a Moko Jumbie without becoming the sun". The Moko Jumbie, a stilt-walker derived from West African masquerade and resurrected in Trinidad's Carnival, sustains the idea of the Jumbie as Muse, magical folkloric guide, who walks on stilts above the ordinary revellers. So the warning here is that one needs to remain, if not rooted to, at least walking on firm ground, even as one aspires to ascend into air, cloud and sun.

One must also transform the stone from its function as barrier into a weapon that one hurls at the blank/void. The idea is derived from Brathwaite's "Negus"[46] where the protagonist calls for "the stone that will confound the void". Such an encounter with the blank is maintained by Questel in a context of extreme tension and implosion where the protagonist tracks:

> The splitting image of struggle,
> the next man's dream in print

The next man's dream and journey, however, are not the narrator's; they only enable the emergence of his own distinctive utterance.

The final phase (?) of the journey begins with Questel's now magisterial command, to himself as much as to Robert Lee: "The slate is dry, /blank. Write". These final lines, an echo again of Brathwaite's "So on this ground /write,"[47] are about the acceptance of mission, and they repeat earlier ideas (e.g. cracks, mist, collapse, the reduction of stilt-dancer to fallen man-crab). Here, the cracked words and syllables are healed by hyphens, disconnection becoming connection. The poet commands himself to "dream", that is, to continue dreaming. There is also that image of the turgid penis that Questel connects with man's (or his own) capacity to (pro)create. Words spurt from his cave of being, after which there is a detumescence, a flattening back into normalcy. "All things that are humped / level to their own/lines."

(10)
"*Near Mourning Ground*"

"Near Mourning Ground", the title poem of this central collection, is Questel's first extended poetic portrait of the "folk" world that he has constantly been skirting in his imagination. It is the first of a sequence of family portraits – uncle, father, grandfather, wife – where family represents not a zone of comfort or the consolation of childhood memories, but a source of the anxiety and an omen of the terror of mental collapse that is Questel's central text. Yet, he must reclaim his family before he can reorient himself. "Near Mourning Ground", in which he paints his memory of Uncle Simeon, a Baptist preacher, suggests through its very name that his careful journey back (or forward) to ground, has begun. Mourning Ground, in Spiritual Baptist ritual, is a ceremony whereby the pilgrim after fasting, ablution and lying for eight days in the "tomb" or "sacred chamber" is, if fortunate, granted a gift from the Holy Spirit and told what his or her life's work is to be.

Questel acknowledges that he is *near*, not *on* mourning ground. He hasn't yet undertaken that dreadful journey in the spirit across land, across water, back towards roots and reclaimed faith. He has, however, moved towards a closer association of his journey with that of an older and even more deeply tired senior generation. Uncle Simeon, stevedore and street preacher, has made a half-inspired, half-doubting journey towards a truth that is less revealed than researched. He becomes a perfect mask for the poet whose typescript, "tightened beneath candle-grease like the drumhead/ of memory", is both the poem taking shape beneath the poet's candlelight of vision, and Uncle Simeon's bible caught in the light of his preacher's candle. Both journeys toward self-discovery are associated with the tightened drum of African Caribbean people which had begun to function as symbol, artifact and metaphor of a whole new phase of West Indian poetry.

Questel's drum is the drum of memory, because on observing a Baptist meeting in Curepe in 1975, he recalls his own uncle years ago in Gonzalez. The performance of the Shouters' meeting is polyphonic, polymetric and kinetic. There is Shepherd's voice; the background chorus of sisters chanting in counterpoint; the interplay of sermon and song; the punctuation marks of the bell; the movements of the congregation which are themselves a counterpoint of swirling circles and staccato jerks; and the accompaniment of handclaps and tambourines. Uncle Simeon, caught in the rhythm of performance:

> swirled suddenly to balance a point on
> time
> to the bell's appeal

Sudden spinning movement and balance are what the Shepherd has and are qualities the poet also needs: balance in the midst of delirium. But as "Words and Gestures" illustrates, Questel is more comfortable with the poetry of isolation than with one of encounter and performance.

This is why his eye is welded to his uncle's movement and the Spiritual Mother's surrender to Jordan River. Both of these extreme acts take him backward in memory to the time when he was a bewildered little boy not knowing what to make of all that passion. Now, as an adult, he intuitively understands that under the drama of shouting and dancing the Word, lie

235

what Walcott in "Pocomania" termed "the sexual fires of Pentecost".[48] He divines that the connection between the Spiritual Mother and Uncle/ Shepherd is as much carnal as it is spiritual, and he recognizes parallels between his uncle and himself. Each is trapped in the chasm between theory and practice, the ideal vision and the worldly reality. For both, truth has become oscillation "between poles of belief", paradoxical interplay of faith and doubt, affirmation and constant questioning. Thus Uncle no longer delivers "visions"

> but a text
> mounted from the lost books of the Bible
>
> calmly prepared the night before by the arc
> of the kerosene lamp;

Spiritual Baptists ideally preach only when directly inspired by the Word of God, their sermons then becoming spontaneous and prophetic utterances under the Spirit. Uncle has become an example of leadership whose original charisma and shining have, with time and the bruise of experience, been replaced by something far more quotidian, even fraudulent. The word "mounted" suggests the obeahtic act of investing an inert object such as the stickfighter's stave with magical power to attack or protect the batonnier. The reference to "the lost books of the bible" indicates that Uncle's text is apocryphal and, in the eyes of the establishment Church, of doubtful authenticity. These "lost books", celebrated in Reggae as "Macabee Version that God gave to Black man"[49] link Shepherd's quest with Vodun, Santeria, Rastafari and Zion Revivalist quests for the lost history and culture of Africans of the Diaspora.

> weekend baptisms
> constantly trying to cross water
> fasting
> eyes covered by several colours of seeing
> reduced,

Shepherd's uncertain journey and pursuit of a lost cause becomes Questel's night journey across water, the dark ocean of psyche. The seven seals or symbolic bandages across the mourner's eyes are also his. Remembering his uncle, Questel gains an epiphany.

> but Shepherd is like any writer
> here
> a lonely pilgrim going to meet himself
> a man burning on mourning ground
>
> grounded by a vision of flight and travel
> heat
> and fears
> [...]
> returned
> and returning to the blank
> page
> trying to speak the vision clearly
> though he cannot
> without a text

Here in this tremendous parallel, Questel engrafts together his quest as writer and his uncle's search for the moment when contemplated text yields epiphanic vision. As in his earlier reference to Watteau's white Creoles who are running from, yet rooted to their island, Questel depicts the Shouter Baptists, Rastafari and similar African Caribbean religious communities as the region's most "grounded" indigènes.

Ideas of escape and flight may well be embedded in the language and symbolism of their liturgies, but their experience of persecution, confronted with fortitude, has indigenized them into the New World as only pain can. Because of:

> ... the private vision
> and the public pain
> the heat and fears
> the stoning of the brethren
> [...]
> they had learnt that here
> it was more important to confront
> Jordan river than to cross it.

This is why despite their obsession with flight and travel, they are described as "grounded"; uncle's feet are "concrete hard scraping the cement". He has become one with the city's grit. The brethren's "retreat to the bush" during the years of persecution from Law and Respectability

237

(1917-1950) parallels the poet's own snail-like journey through undergrowth. What is reality for Shepherd and his congregation becomes metaphor for the poet.

It is with this humbling knowledge that Questel finally addresses the Shepherd, his alter ego, an elder mature voice, possessed of the faith and experience that he lacks, his lost Legba, more grounded in pain.

> Listen Uncle as the sisters hum us home,
> What tract yer pull,
> traveller,
> mourner
> man at the crossroads

What the poet desperately seeks is a tract, also a track, a clear pathway through the labyrinth; a message and healing talisman for his confused mind in this complicated age. In his final appeal, "Lord Uncle say the word", one hears the echo of the Centurion's entreaty as well as the priest's confession of unworthiness before inviting the congregation to Holy Communion. But Uncle, however valid his pain and sermon, has no healing word in spite of the fact that like Eric Williams of the Chaguaramas march, he has been "preaching since the time the Yankees leave the base."

By the end of the poem the poet ascends from his cave of memory and myth. Uncle loses his ritual presence and becomes, like the older male figures in Questel's poetry, a representative voice from the older generation, whose cycle and fable have been perfected. He is "man at the cross roads" in that he is going through the crucifixion of middle age and all its challenges of remembered passion and waning virility, the loom towards extinction. The poet, himself at different crossroads between faith and unbelief, intellect and flesh, seeks to connect his struggle towards faith with that of a defeated, disillusioned but dogged older generation. What he acknowledges at the end, though, is that despite the similarity of the struggle, doubt and defeat that both parents and children encounter, each age, as it senses its closure, "as the sisters hum us home", must seek its own language and trailway out of the wilderness of words and woes.

(11)

"*Father*"

Father, a retired sailor, has been constantly present in Questel's consciousness; and no more so than in "Father," which is about gradual decline, decay, aging, losing balance, memory, mind and finally, life itself. Questel sees himself treading a similar path:

> now I circle
> the fears
> that
> encircled you

He also shares, as he warns his wife, his father's rage as trapped, encircled creature.

> there are rages beneath my
> skull
> that only amnesia can
> cool

At twenty-six or twenty-seven, he is becoming his father in his journey towards wreckage and dotage.

(12)

"*Ash Wednesday*"

In "Ash Wednesday", Questel returns to a familiar trope: the nation as theatre after Carnival. The discarded floats, costumes and rubbish of the previous day's celebration; the drought, bush fires and burning canes, evoke the inevitable homily.

> But that's what this country is about,
>
> the burning of flesh and cane
> the ash
> of effort

Trinidad is perceived as being caught in an endless exchange and contradiction of masks. Its people mock themselves even as they celebrate their contradictions. The same player plays revolutionary one day and reveller the next, thus embodying:

the splintered halves
of your twisted
self-
mockery

The country itself is schizophrenic in its selection of masks; and one had better be certain which mas' is being played on Ash Wednesday, that time of morbid reflection on man's mortality, when mas has gone out of season.

As splintered, twisted and schizophrenic as his society, the poet stands outside of and yet is consumed by the mas. He drinks too much, stares at circles left on the floor by beer bottles and, as usual, feels trapped in those circles. Home is his dark study. He cannot see clearly or swim confidently through the gulf of paper pinned to his wall, the agenda of his inertia. He thinks that his society lacks the sense of dread and profundity that he sees in the eyes of Ras Daniel Heartman's charcoal drawings, which had made quite an impact on Trinidadian avant-gardist consciousness around 1971.

(13)
"Voice"
i: *"Shaka's Cycle: I: A Light"*
It is, nevertheless, with this society of schizoids that Questel begins a new cycle in his continuous quest for voice. An entire section of *On Mourning Ground* consists of oral poems dedicated to Clifford Sealey, Kamau Brathwaite, Rawle Gibbons and Anson Gonzalez. "Shaka's Cycle" is one of the most significant experiments of this group of poems. It is a satire on the rhetoric of 1970, particularly that of Geddes Granger, who was earlier portrayed by Questel as the anti-heroic "epileptic boy of February". Here, wearing the mask of African warrior chief, Shaka Zulu, Granger declaims on behalf of the lost souls of the Middle Passage and blames "dat man" (presumably Eric Williams) for the failure of diasporan Africans to recover direction in the contemporary New World.

dat man is responsible for all that we see here today
We have to deal with that betrayal...

Questel's voice, beyond that of Shaka's, queries silently the notion that reparation of any kind is possible, and the futility of Trinidad and Tobago

240

turning against its maximum leader in Black-versus-Black confrontation. It queries, also, the militant slogans like "Liberty or the Cemetery" or "Seize the Time", clichés borrowed from real revolutions elsewhere. Most comical is "Time Is Tight", the theme song from a then current "Black exploitation" movie, *Uptight*. Shaka harangues:

> When Black people move we
> move as one...

> We know where the guns are

> We know what to do when
> the moment comes

The first statement is palpably untrue, since few ethnic groups would have been, or are, as divided as "Black people". The leader carefully avoids full or even partial disclosure of what he plans to do with the guns that he boasts of possessing (i) because he is aware of the necessity to avoid sedition and (ii) because he has no plans and has been substituting improvisation for vision.

ii: "Burning"
In "Burning", the second section of "Shaka's Cycle", the poem examines the same rhetoric now that the people are on the march, noting, however, Shaka's new emphasis on the ordeals that the demonstrators have had to endure after six weeks of marching up and down in the blistering heat of dry season 1970.

> Remember how the heat lashed our foreheads
> cracked our skulls
> how the hot pitch bruised our heels
> how our hands cut cane. The march goes on.

There still is no news about what Shaka means to do when the marches come to an end. His now tired voice repeats the mantra about "the masses" and particularly the Black masses knowing what to do "when the time comes", and seeks to involve the East Indian community in what he still defines as a Black struggle, with the command (or plea), "Let the hands of Lakshmi/ wave the flags." Lakshmi, as is well-known, has many hands and can be a great boost as flagwoman for the movement.

241

iii: "The Final Flame"

The final flame is about the waning of the movement. Taken together, "A Light", "Burning" and "The Final Flame" indicate the ephemeral nature of the uprising, which bursts like the spark of a struck match, flares for a moment, then splutters out. The guttering of the movement does not quench Shaka's style of rhetorical repetitiveness or alter his devious response to the question of what to do. Shaka's reply after the failure of his uprising is the same as it was at the start: "The fight goes on" – a slogan of the time that used to be declaimed in English or Spanish.

Shaka points to the (soon-to-be) ill-fated guerilla movement as the next phase of the struggle

> Some of the brothers have taken the fight
> into the hills. They have taken the matter
> into their own hands
> and into the hills... Each
> in our own hearts knows what to do.

But the guerilla "movement" was quite separate and different from Shaka's uprising of the urban masses, based as it was on the fragmented initiatives of small clusters of individuals, and on silence and secrecy, whereas Shaka's illusory empire had been founded, as it had foundered, on rhetorical harangue. Shaka's fate was to be detained for several months, while the "guerillas" were hunted down and massacred by the joint forces of police and army, who regarded them as little more than bandits. Such was the brutal reality of things. Echoes of the original illusion can still be heard, however, in Shaka's final mantra:

> We need more black sounds.
> Black people know what to do. We
> have always known what to do. Shaka
> say is the fire next time.

Shaka steals his final slogan from James Baldwin's then current text, *The Fire Next Time*, in very much the same way as "conscious" youth in the sixties had picked up terms and phrases from Fanon and Malcolm X, and their parents had named their nascent steelbands after wartime movies and post-war Westerns. "Shaka's Cycle" – the word "cycle" suggests both circularity and entrapment – satirizes the repeated tendency of Trinidad and Tobago society to build itself on other peoples' melodrama and ingested rhetoric, and consequently to convert a real need for clarity, direction and articulate revolt into cyclic masquerades of futility. On the other hand, for those who justify the Revolution as a sign of the awakening of a whole new generation, Questel's sardonic mockery of Shaka can be seen as evidence that he himself is caught up in his society's habit of reducing honest effort to ash via mockery and parody.

iv: "Scarecrow (for Rawle Gibbons)"

This phase of Questel's poetry represents his movement towards the dramatic. "Scarecrow" is dedicated to Rawle Gibbons because Gibbons had returned to Trinidad and Tobago after a period of intense grounding in Jamaican theatre, and had begun with productions such as his own *Shepherd* and Dennis Scott's *An Echo in the Bone* to expand the vocabulary of ritual drama in Trinidad and Tobago. Gibbons's still nascent theorizing of "dramatic enactments" in Trinidad and Tobago's phenomenal folk-culture, suggested to a questing mind such as Questel's the possibility of an alternative (alter/native) aesthetic to the existentialist nihilism upon which he had for seven years been famishing his own creative sensibility.

Central to the fierce discourse about aesthetic possibilities in "New World", "diasporan", "postcolonial", newly independent, "multi-eth-nic", "multi-cultural", "plural" societies of the Caribbean, was the underlying reality of the Grammar-school nurtured intellectual gaining access to those "censored" regions of his own sensibility – i.e. the folk, folk-urban exploding forms that he had been programmed to erase, or at very best, downgrade, even as he was in the process of thieving them. Questel's work is important because it contains his extraordinary awareness of all of these "crossroads" and "liminal" issues, not as academic concerns, but as the contradictory elements of his own neurosis and tragi-comic drama of consciousness.

"Scarecrow" begins with a tribute to some unidentified ancestor, a survivor like Uncle Simeon, the Shepherd, of processes of testing and harsh initiation. Persistent and enduring, this ancestor has fulfilled his quest. The poet now seeks to "proclaim perfected fables"[50] of his ancestor's life and time.

> He has been horse and river,
> he has been ridden, bridged
> and dammed

243

He has, that is, endured all hindrances, been hemmed in, even dammed (damned?) by every kind of barrier; ridden on one level by the powerful controllers in his society, and on quite another level by the loa, the powers, spirits, gods, the Divine Horsemen who shape his inner journeying. He has been bridged: others have crossed over him, measured his span, travelled above and thus been indifferent to his currents, depths or free flow, his dangerousness, the threat that he poses. Yet he has endured; he is still there, still standing, still uncontained and uncontainable.

> better drummers than you have
> tried to keep him out of
> their inner circle,
> but he is their master
> for he seeks nothing.

He has gone beyond desire, like a Buddhist who has renounced all desire.

In the second 'stanza' there are subtle changes. The subject is now described as having been "river and horse", whereas before he was "horse and river". Now, too, his ordeals are cited in reverse order. "He has been dammed, bridged and ridden / into dust". There is an intensification of voice in this listing of ordeals. This is the reduced man, the hero and quester trampled into dust, skin and spirit flayed to strips, body chastised into vessel for the loa. "You said you mounted him". Is the "you" addressed here an external human controller or a divine horseman?

The answer to this is not clear; but the impact of this "mounting" of the ridden ancestor is that he has lost his voice and become an outcast, banished from all shrines. Dom Basil Mathews in *Crisis in the West Indian Family*[51] noted the tendency among the Spiritual Baptist congregation to fragment over points of doctrine. Uncle Simeon whose faith has tended towards Orisha, but who also retains the persona of a Baptist evangelist, could easily have found himself rejected by both congregations.

He regains his centre and place by building his own shrine and assembling his own flock. A now exploitable target for politicians seeking support from the otherwise neglected and marginalized proles, Uncle Simeon is visited by "that man" (certainly Dr. Eric Williams) whom he endows with spiritual strength and protection and by whom he is betrayed. Here Questel refers to the obeah of politics, one notion of which is that the politician needs to be immersed in powers that can only come through the politician's seeking anointment from the shaman. Inevitably, however, the politician betrays the shaman, or tries to become a shaman himself. This situation verges on absurdity when both the politician and the shaman are charlatans.

In "Scarecrow iii", the betrayal of the shaman as sincere charlatan, by the politician as insincere charlatan, corrupts the very foundations of the already fragile New World community that the politician may be trying to construct and the shaman to redeem. The community now needs to atone for what it has become. Section (iii) describes what needs to be done – rituals of bitter and harsh taste – "to heal / our political sin".

Section (iv) begins: "But you saw it all". The "you" here is Questel himself who is remembering his grandmother and teachers who dreamed "to make dat boy / into a somebody". Questel is, however, despite the hope enshrined in all of his names – Victor, David and Eric – unable to fulfil the dream. He

> ...remained
> a nobody with no dream
> a drifter who saw the lack of
> meaning too early for his own good

Without dream, but possessed of an intuition of omen, he wonders at his grandmother's reduction to dementia, to loss of mind, "voice and vision". Why, he wonders, would God let this sort of craziness befall one whose "hymns would bless the house each morning" of his childhood? Such, perhaps, was the source of his later unbelief, and personal fear of mental breakdown and incoherence; his obsessed concern with voice and vision. He confesses himself "still lost". Growing up has meant only a relay of bewildering memories that began with the wonder he felt:

> ...at the starched
> grandeur of his grandmother's
> Bibled dignity wrapped in yellow, blue and
> brown.

He could not comprehend "her room chalked with cabalistic markings", or her eventual madness.

In "Scarecrow v", education, the ordeal "of lonely toil with /figures" towards examinations that he would fail, has sunk him more deeply into the wilderness, until,

Finally,
an act of trust was
rewarded with a violence
of language
that is still burning
within his skull,
kept alive by its own organic growth
separate from his will

Questel seems here to sandwich all the years of his childhood's wrestling
with words and figures to pass (or fail) examinations; and his later quest
as writer confronted with a different chaos of markings, signs and voices
inside and outside of his head, into a single moment whose climax is a
fearsome epiphany. Words erupt with a violence he cannot control.
Words, that he earlier described as "mad" – (cf "Words and Gestures":
"the words, the words are mad") – seem to have a will of their own.

This may be the vision, the moment of possession by the Spirit, the
Word of God, the moment of "greatness" that his Baptist grand-
mother had to her and the family's disappointment prophesied for her
redemptive son. But this strange anointment – viewed by both Questel
and the family as madness – separates him from the world outside of
his head, makes him mistrustful of the gaze of the Other and leaves him
paranoid. Caribbean people of two or three generations ago had a
healthy respect for education as a major catalyst of self-development
and progress, and an equally morbid fear of the alienating effects of too
much book learning. A product of the yin and yang of education,
Questel, after his volcanic epiphany

...expects abuse behind each eye-lid
each kiss
each handshake.

Abuse is so close to the listerined breath,
he lives in his darkness
alone,
more separate than
any stone

So Questel circles back to his earlier portrait in "Shepherd" of the writer
as "a lonely pilgrim going to meet himself on mourning ground". He is

a writer without community, despite his roots; for when he considers major examples of these roots, his grandmother and his Uncle Simeon, both reduced to voicelessness by the operations of the Spirit, he recognizes alienation as having been a central part of their experience. The rooted seem to be as much in the wilderness, without meaning, direction or coherence of word and vision, as those without roots.

> Yes, he saw it all.
> There is no gratitude there. No
> imagination. Nothing to capture,
> but nothing. He
> saw that blank early and fled.

Yet, ultimately, he embraces Uncle Simeon as Muse and is, in spite of the pointlessness that seemingly surrounds all things, determined to speak "at these cross roads". He ends the poem with the annunciatory words of a Baptist chorus: "There is a meeting here tonight."

V: The Meeting Point

If "Scarecrow" ended with the announcement of a meeting – (maybe of ancestors, memories, shapes or shades) – due to take place in the "tonight" of his soul at the "crossroads" of all ends and beginnings, Legba's and Eshu's meeting-place, "The Meeting Point" is a celebration of words – (perhaps the very violence of utterance, the mad words that he earlier said had erupted with a compulsion of their own: words that had nothing to do with his will).

The outpouring of words in "The Meeting Point", however, is quite controlled. Shepherd's sermon is full of hidden messages. His message to Shaka, rendered in Shaka's rhetorical style, is:

> Tonight you will feel
> POWER
> the ever working Power
> found in the blood
> of the Lamb,
> Amen

Here, Shaka's mantra, the repeated shout of "Power" that punctuated his orations, is being measured against divine omnipotence, and thus human hubris is warned against, though not openly denounced. The politicians, the Catholic Church with its statues and graven images are both termed products of "the wilderness of your bewilderment" and must be avoided or ignored. The "Brothers" from the steelband Crossfire, are advised against being bought out by sponsors from the business world, whose money has become not a form of aid, but of control. Shepherd admonishes them that "only /God is your sponsor/ only he is Life's/ arranger."

In other words, Shepherd speaks to each sector of either his actual or his potential congregation in a code shaped from their own language. Knowing of the ethic of hardness, the fear of admitting any sort of softness and the potential for violence of the young men in the steelband, Shepherd advises them to sublimate hardness, fear of emotion and violence in the music they are making while enclosed under the canopies covering the pans. The Steelband is refuge, an ark of trapped but protected souls seeking grounded destination.

> Noah's ark
> must remain
> your canopy of sound
>
> the flight of tenors
> your dove
> of peace

Shepherd warns against vermin, alcohol, false prophets such as Jehovah's Witnesses (a rival corporation); he also warns against unbelief, which he equates with squatting – the situation in real life that confronts the majority of his congregation. To disbelieve, Shepherd contends, is to be a squatter in a wilderness of uncertainty. It is not to belong or to be legitimately settled in a ground of one's owning or being. The bells, the hymns are part of a ritual of cleansing the shrine of the Crossroads:

> Evil spirits are now cast out
> from the mouth of this chapel,
> the road-side tabernacle,
> this sacred ground
> these four corners and
> the bounding centre
>
> I come with a message

Having created and sacralized the shrine, he now delivers his message directly to the Sons of Ham, "you lost high-strung / ham-strung generation" – high-strung and over-tensed neurotics like Questel himself, hamstrung and crippled like the youth of his time. Shepherd's premonition is of a pool of water turning red. His message is: "Repent". His hope is that a new Moses (Shepherd has long lost faith in Eric Williams) will arise to part the Red Sea once more.

vi: "Good Friday"
"Good Friday" begins with the sound of guns ("Bang/ bang/ bang") replacing the sound of Shepherd's bell ("Badang"/bang/Badang/ bang") and an old-time street crier's announcement that the police (drunken tin-star sheriffs") had beaten-up a would-be forerunner of the Messiah.

> John de Baptist dead

> They beat him in John John,
> his deposit of faith
> lost.
> He broken and beaten

Along with John the Baptist who had the temerity to challenge the Maximum leader in his constituency, a hillside slum overlooking Port of Spain, other victims, opponents of the incumbent régime, have become reduced to Good Friday bobolees, stuffed straw effigies of Judas Iscariot, betrayer of Christ, who is dragged through the streets, hung-up on lampposts and beaten. In Trinidad and Tobago, Judas becomes any politician or public figure that has, according to public judgement, betrayed the nation's trust. In the post-1970 period, however, "Judas" was seen as the leaders (most of them Afro-Trinidadians) of the failed protest groups who became "crucified" national scapegoats, even as Eric Williams's triumphant People's National Movement returned to power virtually unopposed in 1971, and firmly entrenched itself in 1976 when it defeated the United Labour Force, a reincarnation of the devastated Workers and Farmers Party of 1966.

It is not only the Black Power people and the "guerillas", but dissident intellectuals such as those who formed Lloyd Best's New World / Tapia House Movement, that suffer metaphorical castigation and severe mangling.

Here,
every tree reflected their destiny;
men who opened their arms
at the cross-roads
promising a New World
of mud, love, cow-shit and
holy communion
were shot and beaten

Their blood, dropped softly "at the entrance of/every gap and track/in this land", remains unappeased, their rage unexorcised even by "the bell's tongue". A terrible crack has emerged in the ranks of "blackpeople" (as Earl Lovelace terms them). The Shouter Baptists, icons of both a kind of militancy and a passive but triumphant endurance have, apparently, lost their authority (if they ever had any) in the urban boondocks. Uncle Simeon's sermons are powerless to control:

those spirits
that are shooting
more deadly than big John Wayne

Who are these? Residues of Sparrow's "gunslingers" of 1959 or calypsonian Leveller's "delinquents" of 1966?[52] Or are they a whole new generation of gunmen and ghetto gangsters? Or is Questel, in 1976, talking about even more recent resurrections of the dreads, the spirits of those who were "crucified", mangled and detesticulated in the early 1970s?

Questel's narrator assigns to "Woman" the task of cutting down the crucified bodies, wrapping them in coarse cloth and burying them. But he says such interment should be done not with reverence, but with hate. Why hate? Since Isis gathered together for reconstruction the scattered skeleton of dismembered Osiris, and Mary Magdalen, on the third day, visited the tomb of the risen Christ, the ritual role of women has been one of love and reverential care; one of faith, hope and devoted effort to resurrect the body in the case of Isis, or find the already risen Lord in the case of Mary.

But Questel's Trinidad is a place where the rituals have either been forgotten or are debased and deformed. He sees only mockery and hears only the laughter of crows ("Christ, they laughing") in the political cemetery of the seventies. There is no healing here, no reconciliation of generations, either. Questel's prophecy or prognosis was accurate. After Williams's death in 1981:

(1) George Chambers's interregnum foundered.
(2) Arthur Napoleon Raymond Robinson's Nation Alliance for Reconstruction, after an apparently successful reconciliation of fractious elements, became the worst scapegoat/bobolee the nation ever saw, and received more licks and crueler wounds than NJAC or Tapia had received in the 1970's.
(3) Mockery of the harshest kind invaded the rhetoric and songs of the nation's commentators and bards, in a total implosion of that violence Questel had always recognized to be locked within the shell of things.

vii: "Man Dead"
"Man Dead" seems to announce a resurrection, but it is a resurrection of robber talk and mindlessness.

> Gall is my rum
> violence my chaser

This is the text of the unforgiving crucified who, having gone drunk on the bitterness of failed revolution, reinforce bitterness with vengeful violent threat. Their warriorhood is rooted in the tradition of the stickfighter who, when defeated, needed to repair his mask of dangerousness and menace, and thus retrieve his shattered ego. Hence their challenge to any intruder who transgresses into their space,

> Man dead today
> spit
> cross my path
> and
> that is yuh last journey

proclaims their contempt for both their own and their antagonists' lives, and their readiness to kill without thought or remorse. Theirs is a false heroism grounded in degraded ritual, and the violence ingested and exuded by the warrior can only intensify the sacrificial crisis already overwhelming the soul of the nation. Questel's shattered warrior speaks from a limbo state, proclaiming his genealogy and threatening an ominous rebirth:

251

I was that goat
which spawned the first drum

I am that man
who killed Cain
given half a chance
I'll kill you again

The first signification aligns the undead unborn Warrior to the goat in Brathwaite's "The Making of the Drum".[53]

First the goat
must be killed
and the skin
stretched

The Warrior, on mourning ground, is laying claim to this firstness. He was the first scapegoat, the first crucified victim. In the second signification he proclaims himself to have also been the first avenger, the first justifiable murderer. Cain killed Abel unjustly; so, therefore, whoever killed Cain was scourge, avenger. The blood feud, as the Anglo-Saxons and other Nordics found out, though an irresistible and even logically fair system of justice, was also an absurd and wasteful one, that led to an infinite number of killings over generations, and no healing at all. You kill my father, I kill yours, you or your brother kill me, and my brother kills you... ad infinitum until there are no fathers or brothers or families or tribes or people left to kill each other.

To what end has Questel invoked the spectre of vengeance? His Warrior Spirit on mourning ground aligns himself to the tradition of Revenge Tragedy, citing as ancestors both Shakespeare and Webster on the Anglo-Saxon side, and on the African side Shaka Zulu, Coffy (Cuffy), the Guyanese Akan leader of the 1763 rebellion, and Daaga, the failed Yoruba pre-emancipation insurrectionist of Trinidad. What does one make of such a genealogy? Shakespeare, for example, unlike Webster, was a critic of the Revenge tradition and always tried for a vision of reconciliation after the disintegration and mangling of his tragedies. Cuffy and Daaga both failed and were tortured and executed.

A product of such flawed ancestry, Questel's warrior becomes himself an ancestor and teacher of legendary bois men like Massa Hood and Tan Moses, whose protection against demons and curses he can invoke at any time. He also claims, hilariously, to have been "Satan's only horn child/by his sister". He seeks resurrection out of the dimension of Limbo, but has lost connection with spell or spiel of shaman or obeah man, and is forced to become his own shaman and find the ritual words that will lift his spirit out of the deadly torpor of defeat that is its true reality. Meanwhile, from his tomb and jail of spirit he curses, threatens, prophesies future holocausts and even seems to intuit the Islamic genesis of the fire next time, which blazed in 1990, eight years after Questel's death.[54]

> Tajas of crematoriums
> are all you will ever dance now

This ceremony of fratricide, commemorating the slaughter and burial of the Prophet's grandsons, cannot move the lacerated Archipelago beyond the perspective of vengeance or towards healing.

> The moon will be drunk
> with revenge

is still the text pronounced by the Warrior-soul on mourning ground. The poem closes, not with the light of resurrection but with an even more desperate recognition of the reality of the grave as the final prison. The stickfighter's chant:

> Mooma, mooma
> yuh son in de grave
> arready

closes the circle of an anguish unassuaged and unexorcised – this despite the Warrior's claim to life-energies as powerful as those Christ manifested during the Harrowing of Hell.

> I who gave God
> knowledge of Hell
> I who can sweat my
> ancestors' pain
> at will

We leave the poem with this strange paradox of a soul encircled by ineradicable historical pain, who at the same time confronts this heritage of confinement and reduction with an equally unbreakable spirit of fierce and blasphemous resistance.

(14)

"Triangles of Sound"

"Triangles of Sound" is a contemplation of Clive Zanda, Scofield Pilgrim and the Queen's Royal College Jazz Club in performance. As in Brathwaite's "Jah",[55] Jazz music or Jah's music becomes a symbol of the possibility of creating or rediscovering links between the three points of the triangular trade – Europe, Africa, the New World of the Caribbean and the Americas. There are a few places where Questel's reading of and borrowing from Brathwaite are evident, for example: "bridge of sound". Compare Brathwaite's "bridges of sound" ("Jah"); or "your feet float / across the water / of sound". Note the similarity of sensation in Brathwaite's "Shepherd".[56] Questel's "return to roots/water" echoes Brathwaite's "tuned to roots and water".[57]

The echoes are pervasive. Yet Questel traces his own peculiar pathway out of this seeming imprisonment in the trammels of the Muse. Zanda is a "god-man". He is "above the music". He is described as "humped/on top of the music", a Legba hunchbacked figure who "pounds" the keys of the piano. Zanda, whose surname is Alexander, "conquers worlds in his head", like his Grecian namesake, though Zanda's empire is purely imaginary. Converting piano into drum, he sublimates the imploding turbulence of South East Port of Spain, achieving what Shepherd had prophesied needed to be done for the youths of Crossfire steelband to avoid falling into the abyss of fratricidal violence. Zanda seems to sublimate his own rage in the aggressive way that he "attacks" the piano.

> is blows
> is blade
> is chop

These phrases occurred previously in "Clash", a poem that attempted to capture the atmosphere, soundtrack and reality of violence that used to be associated with East Dry River steelbands such as Renegades and All Stars. Shepherd had, without success, warned against such self-destructive violence. Now Zanda, another Legba / Crossroads avatar, illustrates how what Shepherd had advised might be attained. The music, played on an indigenous drum, or in the instance of Pan, a family of drums, could be made into a crucible, a container of the violence of the diasporan African tribe.

Zanda, though, is not playing the Afro-percussive Pan, but the Europercussive piano, and his mission of return to and reconciliation of ancestors is even more complex and challenging than the immensely difficult task of building a bridge reconnecting diasporan and Continental/ ancestral Africans.

> the journey across
> the three points
> becomes
> both pointless
> and pointed
> now

Questel may have returned to his position in "Tom" that there can be no return to ancestral lands or modes of seeing because "the way lost is the way lost". But this resignation to the idea of the pointlessness of the quest is itself counterpointed by Zanda's function as Legba and Pointer (in the Spiritual Baptist church), who points to all junctions and intersections of pathways. "Pointed" may also have another and quite literal connotation: knives, icepicks, switch-blades and cutlasses were at that time, before SLRs and AK47s, important and effective aspects of ghetto arsenals among the young assassins of the New World. This would mean that Zanda's pointing to the pathway is as futile as Shepherd's exhortations at the Crossroads.

Besides Zanda there is the bass player (unnamed, but most likely Scofield Pilgrim), the guitarist, the drummer, an explosive figure ("Hands explode") whose rhythm and energy induce the beginnings of possession, driving the narrator to "the edge" where he balances. We recognize familiar Questel signposts of the internal passage: his sense of being on an edge of light or darkness, of somewhere other than ordinary. The vibrations of the drum enter his head, inducing a sensation of tightening. "The knots in my hair tighten", he says, which can mean that there is no unravelling of the complicated psychological issues with which his "head" is usually beset; no ease in this tension that is prelude to light and life.

> the scalp
> is alive between
> your ear drums

Like Kamau's Shepherd, Questel's feet not only discover ground, but grow roots. It is the bass that, as in "Jah", creates this sense of earth and rootedness. Together, the musicians recreate links between the points of the triangle, if only in dream or imagination. Everything about their music – the melodies "Saltfish" and "Sweet Breadfruit" upon which they improvise, their style and sound, the very instruments that they play – becomes metaphor and invests the listener in search of meaning beyond the surface of performance, with a sense of ancestry, memory and dimension.

To illustrate: Saltfish, fourth grade codfish or pollock, its protein stiffened by deadly white sodium, was a staple food on the New World slave plantations. The calypso "Saltfish" was one of the Mighty Sparrow's risqué celebrations of sex, here centred in the female genitalia, "saltfish" being one of the many calypso metaphors for the vagina. Such sexuality was also part of the affirmation of life through which Africans energetically encountered genocide for three centuries.

Breadfruit was also an imported life-sustaining tree which planters transported from the Pacific archipelago to the Caribbean. Reluctant to allow either space or time to the enslaved, they sought to confront the need for a staple carbohydrate food by planting the fruitful and easy to maintain, once rooted, breadfruit. Breadfruit – a survival symbol since slavery times – is now part of the cultural cuisine in some of the tourism-oriented islands.

Lines and frames, repeated Questel images of confinement, refer in this context to musical scores. So the passage

> Lines take up the slack
> between poles of
> time,

(literally a comical observation of the resemblance between the domestic clotheslines and a musical score with its vertical barlines delimiting horizontal lines) is metaphorically a comment on how the music tightens the linkages between present and past, opening historic memories as the listener's mind plays with the saltfish and breadfruit themes. The Calypso, extended, stretched-out into Jazz – which is what Zanda claimed to be doing – transcends the diasporan and confining theatre of the calypso-tent. The musicians, excavating melodies, create depth and dimension, and the listener/poet becomes possessed by the spirit of the music. His hair "tightens" as he becomes "tuned in" and "turned on".

One recalls the metaphor of attunement in "Pan Drama" where the goal of attunement is achieved only through ordeal.

> The sounds *cut*
> and *scrape* the memory
>
> the bass *bludgeoned*
> stilted
> attitudes
>
> the wise brushes
> *rip* the skin
> till
> knowledge prickles our hair

Jazz music, then, is perceived as a painful, yet triumphant corridor of memory as in Shake Keane's "Calypso Dancers".[54] Here, the cutting of the drum and scraping of the vira (scraper) together with the rumble of the bass, restore the torture, attrition and violence of New World history. Caribbean sensibilities have historically been educated to deny, internalize and swallow pain; to grow tough protective shells against memory of past brutality. A journey backward and downward into memory, therefore, represents a shaking of "the scales off our eyes", a process that resembles a biblical miracle of healing, a restoration of vision after the glaucomic encrustation of historic denial, the cataract of amnesia.

Scales, the sequenced arrangement of notes in music, is forced into yielding a totally unrelated layer of meaning to the poem. The conceit barely works. Jazz music is built on the ability of musicians to violate, twist and break through the prison of conventional (i.e. Western) well-tuned clavier scaling, to release suppressed tonalities and voicings lodged in the "folk" memory of diasporan Africans. Jazz instrumentalists seek atonality, disharmony, the dissonance of the blue note, the cracking of the notes into two or three splinters of sound. Questel celebrates this "shaking of the scales" as a prerequisite for re-entry into suppressed subliminal vision. It is the equivalent of what happens in his approach to the image. He speaks in "Lines" of "the splitting image" as an essential quality of his vision and style.

The narrator remarks that the piano, drums and bass form a tight triangle within the band. They, it is to be presumed, play with a strict consciousness of each other; they "talk" to each other. Is the flautist part of their conversation? Maybe. The flute is an ancestral instrument, associated in Caribbean literature[51] with journeying back into the buried past. The flute's thread of sound tightens the cord connecting the bow and bridge across the Middle Passage. The "triangle" represents a transcension of the purely economic pragmatism that inspired Europe's intrusion via the Triangular Trade into the New World. Questel's triangle celebrates for a brief instant the meeting points of antagonistic ancestors, the intimate and intricate knotting of bloods and cultures in the New World of the Caribbean.

Questel next improvises on the name of the song, "Sweet Breadfruit".

> the fingers of
> the breadfruit leaves
> point us home
> as
> I bleed a milk that
> hardens
> and tries to trap the bird

The leaf of a breadfruit tree is like a strange, huge, curiously-veined hand. Questel reads this hand as another mystical signpost, pointing like humped Zanda/Legba, "the way home". The "milk" is the latex-like sap that oozes from the bruised breadfruit tree. Questel wants to use this hardened sap as gum to "trap the bird". The bird, a celebrated Jazz icon signifying transcension, freedom of flight, imagination and elation, is Charlie "Bird" Parker, an African New World Muse, or John Coltrane in his spiralled ascension, or, since "Triangles of Sound" is about Calypso as much as it is about Jazz, the bird might just be "Birdie", the Mighty Sparrow, who signifies as "the bird with the word" and who sang "Saltfish".

Meditation on the bird prompts the memory that one of the most pervasive birds in Trinidad is not the nightingale or the skylark, a Muse that soars into the sun where it sings, so says Shelley, "Like a poet hidden in the light of thought", but the corbeau or vulture who circles the La Basse or garbage dump, home of stray cats and mongrels. Questel's eye falls on "those cats" scuffling for survival in the garbage. "Cats" too is a Jazz nomen, so one is not sure whether Questel is using cats literally to mean feline predators, or jazzically to refer to the musicians. An aesthetic of the splitting image permits both meanings. Hence the lines:

> The rubbish heap
> is a bird-lime
> that none here
> can escape

hint at the possibility that Sco, Zanda and the QRC Jazz Club may be creating in spite of and against the morass and swamp of the garbage heap, which they don't "escape", though they at times rise above it.

Bird-lime is literally white lime, thrown on the rotting carcasses of animals that pervade the La Basse. But a "lime" is also a gathering of males (mainly) for recreation, conversation and conviviality. Walcott in "The Spoiler's Return" or "The Schooner *Flight*" refers to Trinidad as a "limers' republic", a waste-of-time place. Questel, anticipating Walcott by a few years, equates the lime with stagnation, decay and the capacity to consume and strangle the city's creative spirit. Zanda as "humped" Legba, recognizing the trap of the rubbish-heap, the compelling attraction of the "lime", confronts it violently with "blows", "blade", "chop". As pathfinder he has first to clear and create the pathway through the entangling vines of the La Basse. His pathfinding frees the encaptured somewhat from the shackles of enslavement, gives direction to the questers on their now pointless, pointed journey.

The music now seems to change to a rendition of Nina Simone's standard ballad, "The Other Woman". The narrator initially is not pleased at this change in mood from hard dissonance to sentimental melancholy lament, the feminine counterpart to Calypso Jazz's mask of machismo, cool and insouciance.

> The other woman
> is both a nuisance
> and a
> balance
> a wheel
> a weight

The "other woman" is, perhaps, the Caucasian Muse who had previously dominated the shaping of the Afro-Saxon psyche. She is perceived to be a nuisance now because of the barrier that her imperial aesthetic has been, and still is, opposed to the quest of the New World artist for a suppressed and ostensibly erased "African" self and ancestry. Yet the

Caucasian Muse is also "weight" and "balance" that serve to remind the diasporan Afro-Creole sensibility that it is not only African, but African emburdened and stabilized by something else, a counterweight.

The "other woman" is also described as a "wheel". The closeness of "wheel" to "balance" suggests the Spiritual Baptist concept of a "balance wheel", a crucially necessary stabilizing factor for an individual or society under trauma. "The balance wheel" is also a steering wheel that keeps a ship on course. So the Caucasian Muse (if it is indeed she) is now ambiguously nuisance and stabilizer, an ousted controller who, because she seeks to restore her former dominance, needs to be carefully monitored lest she beguiles the protagonist:

> feel the circle she turns
> on your axis
> look how she angles.

As the narrator nears the end of this dream journey into and through music, he is confronted by contradictory signs: (i) of a belonging and togetherness in dreaming (the bass man, eyes shut tight, seemingly asleep, the pianist "lost in flight", the drummer, high hat fitting tight). (ii) the triangle expanded in imagination to become the Bermuda Triangle, a "trap", "a hole in the sky / in the ocean" – an image not of connecting cultures and world-views, but of the very opposite – the devouring and disappearance of entire ancestries.

> it swallows
> iron birds
> freighters
> liners
> just so...

Or it reduces things to nothing.

> everything
>
> becomes an
> ant-hole
> a crab hole
> a pond
> that breeds
> mud fish

This means that despite all that the dream-traveller seems to have seen and felt, he has returned to void, erasure and swampland perspectives. No firm ground has been regained, nothing has been redeemed, not the past, not the present of blows, blade, chop, red rage, blood clot. He returns to a reality of amnesia and disconnection from both the ancestral past, sunken in the Bermuda Triangle, and the humbler history of his island that no one knows or cares to know. He quits the poem's journey with the wan hope that:

> even now
> 'Saltfish' is taking us there
> to all the old ruins
> the deserted cities
> and villages of this land.

This feeling is counterpointed by his uncertainty as to the real meaning and validity of an experience that has left him "keyed up/ high strung" and still bewildered.

> I have sweated out
> a whole experience
>
> I am returning to stone
>
> lost days
> still
> encircle me

He confesses himself to be "still on edge /but with a greater sense of balance". The music has offered him temporary release from:

> the mud
> the slime
> the gut of all things

and the ambiguity of a history of horror which is also "our hope". While the horror is forever visible and omnipresent, the hope is questionable and well-nigh invisible.

Part I: Looking

Questel's journey on, or in the vicinity of mourning-ground left him no closer to belief. Towards the ending of "Triangles of Sound", it is the musicians, not the listener/narrator, who seem to have been "drenched in the water of their own/belief". The listener returns to stone. The final phase, the last three or four years of Questel's quest, is a journey through "bush" and on pathways hard with stone. The last collection of poems, *Hard Stares,* is divided into four sections (1) Looking (2) The Glare Hurts (3) The Eye Explodes and (4) Cast a Cold Eye. Questel explores the difference between looking at an object or situation superficially and in-depth, or with an intensity and directness of focus.

These poems are all severely shaped. Vision is pain. The "glare" is both the furious look the poet aims at the world, the family, work, life itself, and the harsh blinding flash of light the world reflects onto the eye. The relationship between seer and seen is dynamic, starkly reciprocal and mutually hostile. Throughout "The Eye Explodes" vision is fission as Questel returns to the life-defining experience of cracking-up/breaking-down of the mid-seventies. "Cast a Cold Eye" with all its resonances of William Butler Yeats in his final years and Wilson Harris at the start of *The Guyana Quartet* is, for all its assumption of a mask of indifference, a baleful intuition of death. This entire text of last words is informed by an inexorable severity of seeing.

(1)

"The Bush"

The "bush", a metaphor of a state of mind, "a thicket of things", "a tangle of vines", seems to offer relief from "the harsh glare of rock" Questel receives when he surveys the exterior wilderness of stone returned to after the dream-journey of "Triangles of Sound". The bush, however, offers little respite. It contains images of crucifixion, of "the first tree or thorn" and is just another version of the wilderness, an interior primal space similar to the ones in Harris's *Guyana Quartet.* The traveller who finds himself in this region of the mind has to clear his own pathway through the tangle of vines to make a space for contemplation and clarification. The poet recognizes that if he is to cope with the bush, he will need an entirely different mind-set from the carnivalesque one his society provides.

> You can't masquerade in the bush;
> it has its own rules. Strip to
> the waist and wade through
> a tangle of vines.

He also speaks of men having to clear "their minds of the bush / by entering its pain". So "The Bush" signals a phase of entering pain with the knowledge that the pathway one cuts, the clearing one makes in the thicket of vines will eventually be overgrown once more as "Quietly the bush swallows the cut path." This is a gospel of encounter but not of hope.

(2)
"Dirt"

"Dirt" offers an image of landslide and soil erosion.

> Cracked boulders
> pebbled stones
> rubble of dust
> grains, specks and flints of colour;

This reduction of mountain to rubble of dust is prerequisite to the construction of housing projects, highways, centres of business. The insecurity and instability of the landscape are directly proportional to the security of un/real estate and the solidity of the class of proprietors that control the existence of ordinary people. Yet Questel, staring at boulders as "cracked", as he has time and again acknowledged his mind to be, declares strangely:

> You possess something here. A fleck
> of conscience; something to be
> committed to.

Questel, under extreme economic pressure – rent to pay on the five unfixed places of abode he inhabited during the decade of his writer's life; two children and wife to mind on his low-paying Biswasian teacher's salary, second-hand / third-hand motor car to service and fuel – is more mistrustful of the world of banks and insurance companies than of the shifting soil of gouged-out hills.

He possesses, he says, "a fleck of conscience", implying that the world of high finance, the world of those who control people and the environment, has no conscience at all. He claims to possess "something to be committed to" even as he sees it slip and drain away before his eyes. This commitment carries its price. For if Questel can assert in one line: "Your head is better balanced than their books", he is forced to identify in the next lines with the eroded and disintegrating land.

> It reels with the red dirt
> that comes down with the
> rains…

Balanced, his head yet reels. Delirium and inexorable vortex underlie everything. But as the red runnels (blood of the land) settle to silt and harden into dirt once more, the poet overcomes his delirium. His vision not only settles, gains focus, but hardens, grows more tough; more driven but more stoical; more rigid, and for that reason, more capable of cracking. That vision is all that matters, he concludes. "You can bank on it." With a typical chuckle, he employs a slogan from the world of unreal estate to affirm his faith in his own cracked vision, and his commitment to the non-material and visionary.

(3)
"Hard Stares"
"Hard Stares", the title-poem begins like Brathwaite's "Fetish"[60] but moves in quite a different direction. "Fetish" asserted that by contemplating objects of stone one can restore them to "life", reinvest them with historical or archaeological resonance. Questel seems to echo this sentiment:

> Eyes
> are buried in this bed of rock.
> History is sunk here.

Interment in rock is counterpointed by interment in water, the Middle Passage in which histories were drowned, the sea that for Walcott is history. But Questel may be saying that vision is lost and absorbed, history drowned and irrecoverable in stone or ocean.

The granite of the geological past is replaced by the ribbed red clay-brick of modernity which is, like its predecessor, barren and impenetrable to the gaze. Yet Questel affirms two articles of faith: (i) that hard staring even at surfaces reveals society's class-and-colour social stratification as fragile, unstable "shale" and "jail", mental self-imprisonment; (ii) that hard staring uncovers the shells of lives and civilizations, emptied and dumped; and the lies – "painted truths" by which contemporary societies have lived. Hard staring may be an act of futility, but it does strip away false myths about the past and see through lies in interpersonal and social relations

Under

> the burden of hard stares everything
> collapses. You see fine cracks in love;
> the crevices in ideas. Feel the hair-line fractures
> of your faith

Questel's hard stares are applied not only to history, but to ideas, theories, truths, religion, domestic routine and love. Each scrutinized, reveals its holes.

> myriad of holes surface like your toast
> fixed taut by an electrical flame

This "electrical flame" is the searing glow of vision, the particularity and exactness of perception, the severity of seeing. There is something terrifying here. It is the image (as in "Dust") of things hardening and revealing their perforations. But it is more than this – the ability, like Sylvia Plath, to suggest this drying-out and hardening through the most banal domestic image. Thus an ordinary slice of toasted bread is invested with a latent terror. In "Calm", the final poem of this collection, the pop-up toaster is comically and hysterically transformed into a launcher of missiles.

One wonders whether it is worth the while placing life under such severe, microscopic scrutiny which reveals all the flaws in things; whether it isn't better not to know, or knowing to put to rest some truths or to view them from afar. Some of the poems that follow focus on household objects, intimately remembered relatives. They do camera close-ups on relationships, trying to grasp the concrete and avoid earlier abstractions. But the concrete remains stubbornly "Other", indifferent and impermeable, forcing the eye back into its isolation.

(4)

"Absence", "Housework", "Sheet", "Rent"

Questel in "Hard Stares" alluded to "the fine cracks in love", and one was struck by the fact that throughout his poetry he made few direct references to personal relationships beyond his admiration, awe and fear of his grandmother and his love and sorrow for his father. Both his grandmother and father succumbed to dementia. Questel anticipated that a similar fate lay in store for him. His Uncle Simeon was a powerful example of faith, courage and wisdom on the one hand and an all too human failure to reconcile puritanical asceticism and carnal desire, on the other. There were hints, generally obscure, of his own encounters with women. But most of his personal narrative was concerned with his own mental tensions, his quest for balance, his feeling that he was existentially trapped, his terror of cracking-up, his unrelenting interior quest that few knew about and none seemed able to help him fulfil. He laughed a great deal and saw the comic side of most situations: it was his way of coping with the grimness that he saw whether he cast his gaze on the exterior or interior landscape.

"Absence", employing the domestic image of soiled laundry, paints a picture of the poet's wife via her clothes "thrown aside" and drooping". The picture that emerges of a "dishevelled" female is not flattering, even though a word like "lilt" hints that there is life and sparkle left somewhere in the relationship. Nevertheless, it is disturbing to meet, not the woman herself, but her dirty clothes, "those spaces / – the holes you have vacated", the absence that hints at her presence as seen through the poet's hard-staring, narcissistic eyes.

Yet Marian Questel's portrait of Victor at the Memorial held in May 1983, one year after his death, tells nothing of the ordeal she must have endured, living with him and his illness. She speaks of a man caught up in a frenzy of work that was more important to him than anything else, even his health and maybe his life.

> "Victor's life was dedicated to the arts and the world of academe but he never, even during his last illness, neglected his family. Victor did most of his work at home to a background of household noises and distractions. He often wrote with one hand while nursing a child with the other, and after a long day's work he rarely objected to their romping on his back or to

having to read 'The Three Little Pigs', 'just once more.'

When Victor returned from Jamaica ill, he found it impossible to follow the doctor's advice and stop all work. He was even more helpful with the household chores and spent a great deal of time talking to Sonia and myself about every imaginable thing. He also started work on a new play, reworked a short story and planned out the books and magazines he wanted to publish that year."[61]

In poems like "Housework" and "Sheets", the earlier "Corner Stone" and the later "Severity" we get Questel's "hard stares" version of this dedicated life. A few quotations reveal that it was anything but idyllic. In "Corner Stone", for example, moving into a newly built home is tense with omen:

> The fence
> is up. We will live together here;
> behind drawn curtains, stoned by work.

"Housework" is a dull list of chores which prevent Questel from doing his real work – writing:

> Nothing starts. Quarrels peter out. The garbage
> is wet; it won't burn. Photos of my wife
> are to be taken. Taxes to be paid; scripts to be marked.

"Sheets", like "Absence", which it resembles, is about a frayed relationship:

> Rent;
> torn, bare and split like relationships
> down the middle, these are your essentials –
> sheets.
>
> After years of usage it's like your
> marriage – frayed at the edges
> from too much careful handling.

"Rent" as adjective; "rent" as noun: both spell worry. The sheets bear witness to sexual dissatisfaction and to the phenomenon, celebrated in Jazz, of being alone together, where man and woman, the fence up, inhabit separate prisons in the same house and bed. When Questel stares hard at his marriage, truths are revealed that are unbearable. "More lies have coupled here than/ meets the eye." He arrives at the terrible conclusion that there may be more lies in a simple love-relationship than in the daily newspaper. That's hitting rock-bottom!

(5)
"Downstairs", *"Play Room"*

Playing on the "stares"/"stairs" pun, Questel writes the central poem of the collection *Hard Stares*. It was early in the marriage when Questel, facing a nervous breakdown, moved back into his parents' home in Gonzalez, accompanied by his pregnant wife. There was really no space for him there, and he was forced to live downstairs in an improvised space within the midden of junk and discarded household objects that had accumulated in the "bottom-house" for six or seven decades. Staring hard at some of those objects, Questel, a creative anthropologist like, say, Levi-Strauss, converted downstairs into an image of the past – both the domestic past of his family, the death or ruin of all they had hoped to achieve, and the history of all of his unknown ancestors in the New World of the Caribbean.

"Downstairs" is also the basement of his inner mind, the Id, the dimension of things suppressed but hibernating in the caverns of the psyche. Downstairs reveals to Questel's archaeologist's gaze a wonderful storehouse of images which, though separate and distinct one from the other, are linked through their relationship to Questel, the convalescent protagonist. Downstairs is the landscape of his "madness" the very opposite of the clean well-lighted place that Questel needed for recuperation. Casting a cold eye on the family midden, Questel remembers the journey and failed endeavours of two generations: the adventures in survival of his mother, grandmother, grandfather and uncle. In a dozen broken, rotten and rusting objects, he unearths the efforts to climb up from poverty into gentility: the crumbling piano keyboard, his mother's typewriter, his grandmother's German oven, suggestive, perhaps, of other holocaustal German ovens of his grandmother's time, the myriad symbols of past work, past effort, past survivalism.

Questel recognizes that: "The whole fabric of society is here. Everything." Each object identified seems to be not only a reminder of the life it once had, but an omen of the death that would eventually overtake it. The poet's mission is to make each object tell its history; to expand each narrative beyond its current interment in earth, dust and rust. The German oven, for example, evokes the grandmother, her journey from Barbados through Panama to Trinidad where, after her husband dies, she makes her living, and the family's, baking "the best/bread in the forties North-East of the East Dry River." Note the frontier location, suggesting the upward thrust of C.L.R. James's puritanical upper lower class as it inches its way out of the ghetto. Where has all that effort gone? Downstairs. What has it produced? Only the most modest release from poverty into future cycles of grinding work; the treadmill dance towards nowhere.

If there is any nostalgia in encountering the rusty past, it is dry and unsentimental. Here too, downstairs, the stares are hard.

> Propped against six feet of raw earth
> is a spade without a handle. To the left of this is
> an English typewriter frozen in dirt

Is the *spade* without a *handle* next to a grave-like mound of dirt, a black man without a name? "Spade" was in the 1950s of Samuel Selvon's London, the current street word for all those who were, in calypso-jargon, "blacker than the Ace of Spades".[62] "Handle" used to be colloquial American for "surname". The "*English* typewriter frozen in dirt", symbol of his mother's failed aspirations, may also be an omen of the fate of his own writing, or of the English literary tradition in the West Indies. If the spade, that is, African heritage, remains identityless and propped, stereotypically shiftless black people style, on his own grave which he has, presumably, dug himself, the English typewriter, that is, the other half of the Afro-Saxon heritage, is cold and equally dead.

The "ice tongs" (tongues?) suggest lockjaw, stroke and his grandfa-ther's death, while the words "collapsed" and "depression" are obvious references to Questel's own period of depression and his sense that he was reliving a cycle of mental depression that may have begun with his grandfather. The stiff rusting tongs would then be a sign of his own frozen incapacity to speak under seizure, while his mother's failed adventure as a stenographer is an intimation of his own sense of having failed at the different and more difficult shorthand of modern poetry. Similarly, the "wooden man with a *broken hand for letters*" is his alter ego, his dead double whom he encounters, significantly, "further in". Only the eye of this crippled alter ego is alive and "stares piercingly at you *out of the darkness*." Downstairs is a metaphor for the Id, or whatever dark region of the soul Questel had entered. Since his depression/breakdown of the early seventies, he had been fascinated by both the terror and the creative potential residing in the state of schizophrenia, and he had tried, time and again to explore, understand, contain that blinding force and maybe command it to speak. In "Downstairs", he stares down into that moment, frozen now in memory, when he had known collapse; linking it to scattered objects of a past accumulated beneath his mother's house. The last segment of the poem in which he locates his position, makes this clear. Commenting on his situation as one who also dwells downstairs, Questel says he remains "rather reluctantly" connected to "upstairs" by an electrical extension cord.

> I live below (temporarily) and it's my link
> with civilization. Recovering from nervous exhaustion,
> levelled by junk and objects that define upstairs,
> I, a rusting dog-chain and crawling memory hold
> > downstairs together

He doesn't say whether the reluctance to maintain an electrical connection with "upstairs" and "civilization" is his, or that of his family upstairs who seek to deny any connection to their own neurosis embedded in this son who has (again?) "failed" and fallen down the ladder. Staring hard at his own condition, Questel poses the question of whether society's and civilization's sanity depends on a balance between Superego and Id, or whether in the negotiation that must constantly take place between these two realms of consciousness, what becomes apparent is the tenuous, fragile linkage between memory and denial, sanity and insanity. And though the poem ends on a note of confidence that the poet can and will cope with the task of keeping things and himself together, what comes across is the ever-present imminence of collapse and the severe grace of the effort to stay "together".

Under the considerable wit and dryness of "Downstairs" lies Questel's belief, plain in the last words, that he was being treated like a dog. Staring hard at this brilliant poem, one recognizes resentment beneath its mask and play of wit, along with stoical acceptance of the stony hardness of things. With "Playroom", Questel moves from Gonzalez to Simon Street, Diego Martin, another rented place, where there was the space and privacy vital for nurturing his young family. In this poem, we again encounter Questel's tendency to refer to himself in the second person, as if he were perpetually conducting what John Donne in "The Extasie" termed a "dialogue of one". This habit is pronounced in Derek Walcott's "What the Twilight Says: an Overture" and *Another Life*, where it facilitates the encounter between the poet and the many versions of himself that have existed in his earlier lives.

"Playroom" is unusual. Its subject is Questel's first daughter, though she is never named, and hard staring reveals that the poem is more concerned with the stage props of the tiny theatre that her life has already become, her existence packaged and "collected in cardboard boxes." Beyond the rhymes, the lilting, jingling rhythm that suggests the possibility of delight, lurks a chaos of signs that point to the dreadful, frozen, subterranean realm of "Downstairs". The toys are nearly all broken or cracked. The cracked doll stripping "with wanton abandon" resembles some of the deranged who occasionally undress and walk through the city.

> Raggedy Ann, bent and broken groans
> in the half-light; the sharp teeth of foxes
>
> bare down on two copies of *The Three Little Pigs*

Children's games, toys, fairy tales, the folklore of childhood, mirror a perverse adult universe where innocence will fall victim to savagery of Time, Old Age, Nature and human carnivores. Plastic toy children linking arms against Mickey Mouse parody more adult exercises in survival against the threat of annihilation. Mickey Mouse, Disney's lovable fantasy hero, recalls Questel's earlier depiction of himself as a comic book character imprisoned in the lines or frames drawn by the Comic Artist, who remains invisible and beyond identification.

The poem ends with a small homily addressed to himself, the "you" that now becomes "I".

> I must learn to find love, hi-jacked
> among a rubble of fractured
> parts;
> it's an art my daughter teaches daily

The scenario might change from bottom-house family catacomb to nursery and TV playroom, but the quest remains the same: for order, healing of cracked and fractured parts, and love.

271

(1)

"*Numb*"

The intimation of death is there in the epigraph from Hart Crane who, as Questel knew, committed suicide near Cuba. "Numb", the first poem in this second section, begins with an image of disembowelment in a sentence that uncoils itself only at the penultimate fifteenth line. This gruesome idea of disembowelment is suggested by the sound of a heavy shower at dawn. Normally, the sound of rain when one is securely at home and in bed is one that inspires a deep sense of security and belonging. Questel, however, deeply insecure and paranoid, finds as little comfort in dawn as Eliot's Prufrock finds in evening which suggests to him "a patient etherized upon a table". The external world becomes a projection of his interior neurosis so, at dawn:

> The sun cuts
>
> through to your [i.e. his] figure
> shut in from the numbing
> pain that heralds another seizure.

He is shut in, yet not insulated. The sun cuts through to his figure "shut in", imprisoned, isolated, huddled, locked away from, yet vulnerable to the pain of another seizure. He comments on "his bitter mirth", which is what his whimsical humour and light-hearted word play reveal themselves to be under close scrutiny. Again he muses on the figure of his father, locked in a cracked amnesiac silence

> ...an outcast sailor
> who traces with his finger or dead butts
>
> an ashen path along a concrete
> bannister that ants have crawled before

A recurrent figure in Questel's poetry, this dotard sailor is the double of the poet, whose writing will also be the trace of an ashen mark on concrete, a madman's faint doodle, invisible as the imprint of crawling ants. He portrays himself as:

> lucid, comical, conceived

and foresees his own death in his father's imminent demise: "The sailor's dying: hear the bang of his door."

Crack-up, then terminus; life ending with a bang, not in the sense that the father rages "against the dying of the light"[63] but in the sense that death slams the door on life. The unasked questions that arise out of this unsentimental portrait of father and son are whether these little grey lives are, whether *any* life is worth anything. How does bitter mirth help one to cope with what Teilhard de Chardin once termed, "the passivities of diminishment?"

(2)
"Pa"

Thus introduced, the father is now portrayed in full detail. No outcast here, he is "in the quiet of the dining room", "an ageing man… huddled over scrambled eggs." But a Questel dining room is likely to be as sinister a stage as his daughter's playroom and Pa himself is an ambiguous omen. For example, "the silent rage of his broken posture" suggests that this dotard with "the *Guardian* drooling from his hands" was once a figure of some power and authority within the family. He is now diminished, trying but unable to maintain a grasp of things or to fulfil an earlier role of "guardian" of a family he once tyrannically ruled between voyages.

Pa has long ceased to be an angry, stern, unsmiling, dapper young man in control of anything. "Blanks circle him". That is, he is beset by a sense of both void and entrapment; "blanks" here having the additional connotation of amnesia or loss of memory. He remembers things in part and in snatches. He has his fixed narrative of a roisterous youth "when he rolled and pitched / the seas with the best", like Captain Cat, the old sailor in Dylan Thomas's *Under Milk Wood*. Maybe his rolling and pitching were an allusion to drunkenness, maybe to wild encounters with equally wild women. (Yet he seldom laughed in those days of gaiety when he felt more anger than joy).

In his yarns he paints an image of himself as committed to the fundamental things of life. He established foundation stones for the house he built. He had a "fixed drive", determination, direction – a man with stones who knew both what he was building and where he was

273

going. He held the strain and sacrificed for his children to ensure that they would not have to go through the same sacrifices. Yet he seems to regret the sacrifice he made and the ease his children enjoy. The still self-righteous Pa tells of "the strain of sacrifice his children never held" to a son who sees his own life as one of sacrifice and holding constant strain. It is an irony Pa will never perceive. For,

> ... dazed by so much thought and recall
> the aging man keels over. Almost bent double, he's
> anchored to his eggs.

"Pa" is the final portrait of the patriarch overtaken by Time and reduced by the vicissitudes of change to impotence. He was there in "Sea Blast" and "Father". This final portrait differs from the one in "Father" in one significant respect: Questel in "Pa" excludes any hint of his own terrified self-identification with his father's disintegration; while in "Father" he had made explicit the parallel between his father's condition and his own. This effort at detachment is characteristic of *Hard Stares*. It indicates not increased distance between the poet and the life or dying he observes, but rather the imminence of his engulfment in that life. It is because of this that the lines of the portrait in "Pa" are harder, bleaker, more dry; that no softness is allowed to mollify the severity of seeing and depiction.

Questel lays on his reader the responsibility of gazing more deeply into the portrait to reveal the empathy he feels for his father. We noted the parallel between the father's aimless doodling on the concrete bannister and the poet's view of his own scribal efforts as making futile marks on the hard opaque surface of life. The sailor, feebly domesticated and anchored to his home, is forerunner who is similarly protective and huddled over his family, though uncomfortable with a domestication that thwarts the manic frenzy of his drive to work and struggle towards excellence.

The "silent rage" of his father's "broken posture" is also the son's. Father, like son, now sits at the centre of an encircling void; the father a memory away from his sailor's days, the son similarly separated from his boyhood when, like the father, he pitched and rolled (marbles) with the best. Both stand at the centre of the same circle, dazed from thought and recall; and although Pa remains to the end almost a stranger – he is still referred to as "the aging man" – and although the son retains the apparent distance of a narrator, there is final recognition and embrace. For surely the words "almost bent double" are meant to convey two distinct meanings. There is the visual portrait of the old man, "head and feet coming together in life's pilgrimage" like Wordsworth's Leechgatherer, a living hieroglyph of the life's cycle he has almost completed. But the ageing man is also the poet's almost bent *double*; his alter ego, the father whose predicament the son silently shares.

The tie between father and children is finally affirmed in the poem's last words: "he's anchored to his eggs" which return us to the image of domesticated sailor and recognize the father's secure rootedness in the nest of a family he has engendered. In staring hard at his father, Questel stares at his own future. Hence he closes the poem with gentleness and acceptance, and resignation that anticipates the final laying to rest.

(3)

"Aunt" is a brief sketch based on a memory of one who has been dead for more than twenty years. Four things are recalled about Aunt. (1) She made funny noises in her throat and called it thunder. (2) She explained her noises as being God talking to the animals, or rearranging chairs. (3) She would then roll over and play dead. (4) Her drama ends when, silenced by real death, she no longer needs to *play* dead.

Is the poem simply a portrait of Aunt? Hard staring suggests otherwise. Her "funny noises" and weird explanation of them are the poet's first exposure to the absurdity of human statement and the tragicomedy of human action in which life, shorn of its primal energy (thunder) is no more than practising to play dead in a landscape deserted by its Creator who "has stopped talking to the animals" (including mankind) and presides over a universe of broken furniture. The heartbroken child laments the dead aunt; the poet laments his disconnection from the Creator, his inability to access the thunder of language in a landscape of broken furniture where human or divine sounds have become reduced to "funny noises".

(4)

"Pathway (In Memory of Mark)"

"Pathway" is an elegy for Mark, a baby boy who lived for only a few months. He is commended for having gone through his life's cycle in a short time, rather than lamented as one who has gone too soon.

You did in weeks what takes

some of us a life time, silently
lisping from cradle to grave.

Here, man is viewed as frail and inarticulate with death as his most cherished and desired achievement. Mark becomes a pathfinder whose death warns the living of the inevitability of their own.

Onlookers

worried about the location of your bed
of rock. You smiled off their concern
as your tiny arm cut a path-way

that they shall follow to that door

Who or what in obeah mythology is this smiling dead (perhaps undead) child? Is Mark a gentle or a sinister pointer of the way when viewed behind his mask of lisping, dying child?

(5)

"*Accident*"

"Aunt" and "Pathway" are deceptive little poems that reveal potential complexities under their smooth hard surfaces. "Accident" is openly grim and full of pain. A woman stands on the bridge. Her "faith is haemorrhaging"; she is "desperate" and willing to "take anything/to get to the other side/ of town." Seeing through the ambiguity of the language, one suspects that this woman is contemplating suicide. She steps in the path of a moving car and is broken and mangled. Yet it is not the wreckage of her body that is shown, but the destruction of the car, which is described as if it were a person, suggesting the reification of the woman and the humanization of the machine.

What is "hard" about the gaze in "Accident" is the apparent objectivity and dispassion of the eye as camera. The poet conceals his compassion, though words like "haemorrhaging" and "desperate" and reference to the woman's aching thighs are clues to his helpless concern. Why is she bleeding? Pregnancy? Troubles related to the womb? Has she been raped and abandoned? What is, or who is responsible for her loss of faith, her desperation? Loss of faith in whom of what? God? People? Life itself? She is willing to "*take anything*". Ominous words. Is she a prostitute who, abandoned after some gruesome encounter is now desperate to return to a less perilous side of town? The poem doesn't say. The reader must guess at and invent his or her own explanation from the clues provided: the devastated woman, the bridge between wilderness and somewhere else that is termed "*the other side of town*". Are we dealing with yet another allegory of the Questel quest?

(6)
"*Paper*"
"Paper" marks the end of the second of the four sections that make up *Hard Stares*. It illustrates Questel's peculiar ways of gazing at and writing the phenomenal universes within and outside of his head. The "hard-stares' way of looking seems to require two things: (1) an image that is first clearly, but superficially perceived – a dear aunt who makes funny noises in her throat, likes to play dead and eventually dies; a baby whose language is a lisp and who dies smilingly; a perhaps violated woman abandoned on a bridge outside a city, who hurls herself in the path of a moving vehicle and is killed. (2) These superficially perceived images when placed under "close scrutiny" reveal crevices, strange alignments with unexpected implications, that lead to dreadful epiphanies.

In "Paper", the superficial image appears when a frustrated school boy abandons a map-reading test-sheet on volcanoes, twisting, turning, squeezing and crumpling the paper into a ball that he will eventually commit to the rubbish bin. On the test sheet are contours, mountain ranges and a ring of volcanoes. The act of crumpling the paper into a ball breaks up and realigns the contours into a crisscross of lines and a succession of crevices. One can no longer derive direction from this map which has become its own New World, a flawed man-made version of the globe.

Under close scrutiny, "Paper" is about loss of shape and direction, cracking and crumbling; the pain of being twisted, turned, crazily realigned and even "transfixed" into unfamiliar and uncomfortable postures. There is need for a new map or for new eyes, endowed with the capacity to read this new lopsided ball or globe. There is also a loss of fire and explosive energy as the old volcanoes burn out or simmer down to ash. As in "Downstairs", the whole fabric of New World experience is here. "Paper" hints at the disruption of old cosmogonies in the creation of the New World by a Maker who, disgusted by the imperfections of the world he has created will one day crush and consign it to a rubbish bin of

277

flawed, failed projects. The Creator of the beginning is the Destroyer of the end. So "Now a bin yawns wide to receive a world."

The crisscrossed lines and new triangulated positions that in "Triangle" were offered briefly as challenge and hope for a brave new world, are here signifiers of an aboriginal chaos from which neither the New World mind nor the New World itself, has recovered. Both are the result of the Creator's unfinished and abandoned exercise. As the ball of paper becomes "entangled in its own crevices", so does the poet's mind realise its entanglement and its cracking into crevasses; the "encrevassment" – (if such a word exists) – of the psyche, whose final destination will soon be the yawning rubbish bin, man's fate.

Part III: The Eye Explodes

(1)

"Judge Dreadword"

The eye / gaze epigraph is taken from W.B. Yeats. "Come fix upon me that accusing eye./I thirst for accusation." The focus of Part III is sociopolitical. Forbes Burnham, the Prime Minister of Guyana, is the subject of two of the poems, "Footfalls" and "A Prime Minister's Address". Walter Rodney, victim of an assassination of which Burnham has been accused, is the co-subject of "Footfalls". "Taking Orders" examines the emergence of militarism and the robotization of the military menial, a growing feature of the post-Independence era in the new Caribbean. Assassination, the emergence of the police state, the growing possibility of coups d'état, these are perhaps situations that might bruise the eye that perceives them, and open questions of attitude in the face of atrocity.

What stance should the writer, be he poet, journalist or both, assume? Empathy? Indifference? Involvement? Disconnection? Who is guilty, who innocent, who responsible for the imploding Caribbean societies as they crumble inwards, or the exploding ones as they seem to fall apart? Who are the accusers, who the accused? If the Trinidad Black Power volcano had burned itself out by 1980, what was the meaning or implication of the fearful turbulence in Guyana from the Black Friday of 1962, to the assassination of Walter Rodney in 1980?

Those are some of the issues raised in "The Eye Explodes". But Part III does not immediately confront this grand theatre of dismay. "Judge Dreadword", its first poem, is a merry satirical parody of Prince

Buster's, "Judge Dread", the first of a trio of reggae songs about a Jamaican judge who tried to stem the rising tide of urban gangsterism by sentencing Kingston's rude bwoys to long jail terms together with corporal punishment (lashes, licks). Prince Buster caricatures the Judge, a worthy Afro-Saxon gentleman, and exaggerates the sentences that he pronounces – "I sentence you to four hundred years and five hundred lashes." Or, "Just for talking I now charge you with contempt, and that is a separate hundred years".[64]

Questel's Judge Dreadword, too, is a powerful defender of old colonial traditions and aesthetic standards, and an aggressive and dismissive critic of most of the new writers who had begun to discuss the validity of what was being called the alter / native tradition. Rude Bwoy Q mounts his own defence as he absorbs the accusing gaze of the irate Dreadword. He shamelessly confesses to being a purveyor of the pun for whom surprise is a lethal weapon, and a destroyer of conventional modes of poetic style. Dreadword accuses Q and others like him of corrupting and violating language and of not having paid their dues to the great wide (white) world of letters. He stresses the power and importance of the court he represents.

> This court is a product of a proven tradition
> of oil and its related cultural benefactors –
>
> BP, CIA, IMF, IOU, the UN, PNM – letters that matter
> in the world. You want to destroy all of that? Hush up.

"Hush up" is the frequent interjection by which Prince Buster's Judge Dread denies his Rude Bwoy defendants the right to speak in their own defence. He also passes sentence on the attorney for the defence for defending Black men who have committed crimes against the Black race. Dreadword commands the defendant to "Hush up" in order to censor the expression of an emerging generation and to defend the consolidated interests he represents. In the process of exposing the bases of his authority he reveals the link between imperialist control of word and image and imperialist exploitation of the world's material resources. The fruits of such exploitation are used in the metropole to subsidise a complaisant Art that says the correct things, avoids political confrontation and challenges nothing. Literary acclamation is under the control of Dreadword's court, where deviant young writers (and nations) are routinely sentenced to four hundred more years of colonial servitude, in the same way that international Capital entangles their economies. IMF = IOU.

Judge Dreadword, like his forerunner Judge Dread, is authoritarian, dictatorial and contradictory. He brooks neither silence nor dialogue in his court. He accuses and passes sentence in the same breath. Affirming the precedent set by Herod, the High Priest and Pontius Pilate, the united hierarchy of the colonised and the colonisers, he announces his final punishment: crucifixion. Yet he fails in the end to stop the drive of younger writers towards independence of style and freedom of choice. Rude Bwoy Q remains a rebel against authoritarian structures and strictures, even when he seems most to acknowledge them.

(2)

"*Shop*"

Like "Judge Dreadword", this is an apparently light-hearted poem, though the imagery – Koo farting in the corner as if in response to his customers; or chopping and weighing meat like a skilled executioner – points to the presence of the usual harshness, asperity and acridity beneath the surface of the poem. Is Koo, for example, another alter-ego for Q? Does Koo nurture a dream of power and violence as seems at times to be the case with Q? Is Koo, like Shylock, striking back at a racist community that marginalizes and demeans him? Note how "Meat swings *in the balance.*" Is Q, like Koo, silently keeping everyone's account and waiting for the day when everyone will pay? Koo, like Q, "does not trust the rumours of prosperity." The difference is that Koo is, in his small way, part of the commercial system he mistrusts and can, unlike Q, "out off" when he spots the opportunity.

Koo lives in and on the society, but is not of it. When he leaves, "Ram gets wind of it." Is the wind Ram hears of (smells?) the same as the "broken wind in the corner?" That is, had Koo's business been failing all the time? Ram, the Indo-Trini, stereotypically, like Koo, attuned to the art of making a business succeed, establishes a VEGETABLE DEPOT – (note the pretentious Biswasian lettering) – which, despite its policy of 'No Credit' seems to be failing as well. The final comment of the village survivalist who, owning nothing, has been the typical customer of both Koo and Ram is: "Lard; life dread."

This is a poem about racial profiling. So we see the smart, secretive

Chinese; the Indian who succeeds him and who is just that little bit less smart; the 'Creole' customer/consumer/ survivalist, ultimate downbeat product of succeeding cycles of hard times, never owning anything to either build up or run from. Beneath the surface of this taut, witty narrative and its laughter, this reader, staring hard, suggests this hopeful/hopeless scenario: Koo, Ram and Q will all eventually end up in Toronto, where other people swing the meat, balance the books and sell the ailing vegetables.

(3)

"Coup or the Hopeless Art of Writing"

From Koo and Q to Coup!! The stage here seems to be Jamaica with its marijuana trade with Miami and atrocities such as the burning down of the old women's home, Eventide (while the old women were in it). The stage could also be elsewhere in the Caribbean Basin. The narrator is a concerned local journalist, aghast at the multiple signs of atrocity and social disintegration in his country. Yet, his dismay is expressed in the hard, cold, "objective" tones of the professional, trained not to let his feelings interfere with his reporting.

The narrator recognizes that in his disintegrating world the coups happen more regularly than there is time to record them. Coups are perpetually breaking news; drama/melodrama for the international media, who are on the spot to film each event almost before it happens. Parochial concerns such as questions of conscience or feeling are irrelevant to the media, for whom bad news – the more melodramatic or horrendous, the better – is simply good business,

The narrator experiences a great powerlessness. He can neither prevent nor narrate the coup. His country is under the new imperialism of the Media, the Mafia and other major manipulators of the drama of chaos and unrest that has become the norm in his society. Recognizing his helplessness, he considers the equally futile option: to "burn with rage and stage the coup myself." This is the only way that the Caribbean person can become the subject of his own social tragedy.

(4)

"Footfalls (In Memory of Walter Rodney)"

This poem seeks to explore Rodney's transition from academic historian to activist seeking to make, or significantly determine the direction of history, even if this results in his death. The I-narrator here is an extension of the frustrated journalist of the previous poem who, staring hard at his powerlessness to shape the future of his own society, considers the prospect of expressing his subjectivity through rebellion. The Rodney persona has long passed that phase. He is absolutely clear that "Action is what is left." Politicians, that is talkers, equivocators, rhetoricians, "can have the rest." That is, politicians can, (as David Rudder was to say seventeen years after Questel's death, in *The Ganges and the Nile,* (1999)), say and do whatever they please). Questel's Rodney has said goodbye to all such irrelevance. His tragic choice is an individual and absolute one, based on his personal recognition that:

> History is not found in history books,
> It is the here and now – meaningful departure –
> if it comes to that.

This is the hard conclusion of one who has stared hard at "history", the written record of past action, and politics, the masquerade of rhetoric that conceals or excuses current paralysis.

There is, however, no space for action and little meaning in the death that results from action. Rodney is assassinated and the "action" that he took, together with the crushing retaliation it catalyzed, have become the very fiction of the news media that so enraged the protagonist in "Coup".

> News time;
> a nation footfalls down waterfalls of silence.

The nation who had never really been involved in the Rodney movement or concerned about the complex of inner forces that had impelled him towards absolute sacrifice, greets the shocking news of his assassination with silence, not outrage. They are imagined by the narrator to be descending Wilson Harris's mystical waterfall[65] shying away from whatever nobility is associated with ascent.

The poem closes with two contrasting images of the Guyanese dictator. He manifests first as a self-anointed and self-righteous obeah man whose seeing eye foresees and forestalls revolt and whose shamanistic voice threatens to confront rebellion with Ogun's fire. He finally is most memorably projected on the television screen in an interview with Trinidadian journalist, Neil Guiseppi, where the camera's accusing stare reveals the crevices in the dictator's mask:

282

> A dictator is turning to ashes in his chair
> while trying to outstare
> both a camera
> and the sad truth of murder.

Derek Walcott in 1969 recorded his impression of Guyana in the aftermath of the holocaustal civil war of the early to mid-sixties, as a morally collapsed nation caught-up in a game of denial that he described as "outstaring guilt".[66] Just over one decade later, the moral collapse of this, since 1966, newly independent but already demoralized nation, is reflected in the stony face of its political leader, who is judged, condemned and executed by the camera's accusing eye. His executive chair in which during the interview he kept turning from side to side in semicircles, is transformed in the narrator's imagination into an electric chair.

(5)

"Taking Orders"

"Taking Orders" is a satirical portrait of the military, that crucial component of any dictatorship. Located between two poems that focus on the burgeoning Guyana dictatorship, "Taking Orders" depicts the ossification of the armed soldier who willingly becomes the pure instrument of his commander's will.

> He longs to
>
> turn to stone, to
> be a living monument
> to his people. He
>
> will stare from the
> heights of some cenotaph
> at a museum of
>
> lost artifacts, bones, shells
> and shell-shocked men.

A nation mummified, its military ossified, creates the perfect context for the emergence of the dictator. Zombified, the soldier "drowses over his butt" – (both gun butt and buttocks). He is startled into life by the order "Attention!" The zombie awakens from stupor at the shaman's command.

> He stiffens as he
> realizes his dream

The phallic pun reduces the soldier to the rank of a wet-dreaming greenhorn. Beyond his neophyte's dream of becoming a national hero, "a living monument / to his people", lies the reality he may well experience, of becoming, like the armies of dead unknown soldiers memorialized in cenotaphs and memorial parks throughout the Archipelago, an object of inert stone. His dream of becoming a *living* hero might reach its zenith in his transmogrification into dead statue, staring at the indifferent or gawking world through dead eyes.

A worse and ultimate reduction awaits him: to become a mere artifact like the bones and skulls displayed in the museum that overlooks Trinidad's (and Guyana's) war memorial(s). This is the final state of a zombiedom that began when he surrendered his will to the commander: a zombiedom from which no shaman can awaken him.

One unanswerable question that emerges from this poem is whether the soldier's surrender of will to the idea(l) of blind loyalty in the patriotic cause of national security, is different from Rodney's willed choice of self-sacrifice in the cause of creating his dream of a new society. Are all causes, however noble they may seem to be, cracked? Is all great dreaming subject to what Joseph Conrad terms "the degradation of the idea?"[67]

(6)

"A Prime Minister's Address"

We last saw the Prime Minister turning from side to side in his executive chair, trapped in his circle under the camera's relentless unequivocal eye. Transported by the omniscient narrator inside the head of the Prime Minister, we heard his vow to eradicate dissent by using the force(s) at his disposal. "A Prime Minister's Address" deepens the portrait of the dictator by amplifying the sound track of his soliloquy. The first surprising truth to emerge is that the Prime Minister of the *iron* will is the corollary or obverse side of the soldier turned to *stone* for having surrendered his will to the commander's. Both men have dehumanized themselves. The soldier becomes one kind of robot, the Prime Minister, stoned with work and the immensity of what needs to be done to achieve his dream of developing the country, becomes another.

The people, too, develop "iron stares", a hard dead blankness of vision and a dumbness that mouths the Prime Minister's "opinions when I give it to them". The Prime Minister utters hard truths about postcolonial development and its paradoxes; where to progress in one direction is to retrogress in another. He also simultaneously confesses and deflects the blame for his own moral failure. He too is entangled in the ironies of "sacrifice". He is an alienated man, reduced to his guards whom he can't afford to trust and who don't trust each other or him. The Prime Minister's suspicion and fear is that not all of them have become zombies. "They too have a destiny to mould". (*A Destiny to Mould* [68] is the name of Burnham's collection of essays). The irony is bitter and bitterly savoured. He has produced robotic effigies of himself. The people, trained like the soldier to echo the leader, become amnesiac whenever they are forced to look him straight in the face. There are

> regular blackouts
> when they see the whites of my eyes.

The "blackouts" are both the electricity cuts that the state regularly inflicts on the people and the failure in memory that the people pretend as they passively accept or resist the system. The "whites of my eyes" suggest that the Prime Minister shares the same way of seeing as the white people he has replaced, some of whom are underwriting his corrupt régime. The last few lines make it clear that the PM's address isn't reaching the people who have long learned to immunize themselves against such toxic nonsense. The political meeting which the people are coerced into attending is an occasion of mutual non-communication, where any hard-staring observer can perceive the lie of the land.

(7)
"Genesis of the Clowns"
"Genesis of the Clowns", named after a story by Wilson Harris, is a poem built entirely on allusions to the fiction that either foretells or anatomizes the dire state of Caribbean post-independence politics and culture, "fates and freedoms". Long before Burnham begins to mould and manure his dream of development, the writers have foreseen a destiny overtaken by mould. [69]

The first allusion is to C.L.R. James's anatomy of Melville's *Moby Dick*, *Mariners, Renegades and Castaways,* (1953), recently republished after a generation of invisibility. Two of these groups, the mariners (i.e. the leadership class or caste of professionals, men-on-the-make, who are now responsible for steering the ship of state) and the renegades (that is rebels, revolutionaries, subverts who question and object to how and where the ship of state is being sailed) have in their interaction created the bacchanal/masquerade "whale of a time" and the drunken brawl that social life has become.

"The stilled eye of the globe" is a sign derived from Harris who in *The Guyana Quartet,* especially *The Far Journey of Oudin*, presented the eye of the sun as a symbol of cosmic justice, retribution, a higher order or scheme of seeing (like the humbler camera in "Footfalls"). In Questel's "Genesis of the Clowns", that eye of conscience, guidance and judgement is blinded and the inner voice is shut off. It is a global condition, though most glaringly evident on the parochial stages of small insular recently independent states. With the next two lines:

> the river of time shifts its bed to
> dance a riot of colour

we are still in the universe of Harris iconography. Here, the imagery speaks to the interruption and change in the direction of New World history after the catastrophic intrusion of Columbus and the conquistadors; the alteration of lifestyles, the emergence of "a riot of colour"; that is, the turbulent, hybridized and traumatized societies, existing in bacchanalian situations. It is these carnivalesque societies, characterised by both riot and dance, murder and masquerade, that Questel terms "the clowns". The next two lines are inspired by Naipaul's *A Bend in the River:*

> up river
> there is a bend all right

Naipaul's intense judgemental eye sees through the riot of colour and the dance of clowns to their genesis in the barbarity of conquest, racial confrontation and genocide. Set in a contemporary African country *A Bend in the River* is a dispassionate anatomy of postcolonial chaos that involves not only the internecine confrontation of ethnic communities/tribes/nations of Africa herself, but marginal Asiatic commercial communities and a scatter of European mercenary, missionary and professional experts and adventurers. This drama of predation is enacted against the backdrop of the 'bush' and the river: primordial agencies that retaliate against human efforts to shift their beds and alter their flow.

Questel's focus shifts to the contemporary Caribbean, Trinidad in particular, where the beginnings of the worldwide recession of the 1980s were manifesting themselves in "a waterfall / of currencies" that succeeded the over-inflated financial ethos of 1970's "Oil Boom". The Oil Boom had created new stilt dancers, carnivalesque mokojumbies, predators masquerading in the dance of money and politics and ultimately, banditry and bloodshed ("painting the country red"). This is the world that Koo perceived and fled and that Q had always feared and rejected – the world of the "clowns". He intuited, but did not live to see the bloody, ruinous climax of the eighties in the 1990 uprising with its "tadjahs of crematoriums".

The final lines of the poem refer to Lamming's *Natives of My Person*.

> A *Reconnaissance* sails down its bed of lime stone
> In that reburial – genesis

Natives of My Person tells of an attempt to create Utopia out of a New World that has already gone awry through conquest, genocide, enslavement and the implantation of malignant Old World feudal and hierarchical structures. The *Reconnaissance*, flagship of the Commandant and would-be founder of Utopia, is an ambiguous symbol. The new vision, the knowing-anew that it envisions, proves terrifying to the Old World minds who dream of renewal but cannot transcend the errors, perversities and atrocities of their past.

Yet Questel envisions the possibility of genesis through and after "reburial". Reburial, a concept that emerged through one of Don Drummond's compositions, seems also to relate to Harris's central idea in *Palace of the Peacock*, of the soul having to live through several cycles of purgation and endure several deaths and rebirths before it can experience renewal. Utopia, then, is possible and may even be inevitable, but not here, not now, not in this dying cycle of time: these collapsing times.

Part IV: "*Cast a Cold Eye*"

The title of this final phase of Questel's intense journey and quest, derives from Yeats's magisterial command that the following epitaph be chiselled into his gravestone.

Cast a cold eye
On death on life
Horseman, pass by

Wilson Harris uses Yeats's epitaph as the epigraph for *Palace of the Peacock*. Questel's appropriation of "Cast a cold eye" relates to his reading of both Yeats and Harris and his preoccupation with the images of "eye" and "stone"; that is, with intensity of vision and the opacity of the visible universe from which meaning is vainly sought.

Read in the context of *Hard Stares*, Questel's casting of a "cold eye" reaffirms his painfully attained posture of stoical indifference in the face of both the absurdity and the terminality of existence. Such indifference virtually negates the glimpsed possibility of genesis that emerged at the end of "Genesis of the Clowns". Little of Questel's poetry supports a philosophy of rebirth. If anything, the cycle of renewable life is portrayed by him as a trap in which mankind is entangled. Camus's Sisyphus,[70] recognizing the ordeal of eternal repetitiveness to which the Gods have condemned him, proffers lucidity and scorn as means of surmounting this anguish. Questel does not accept this. For him, to be lucid, as he in "Numb"[71] declares he is, is simply to have a clear perception of the trap in all its forms and disguises. The beginning and end of the cyclic human situation is the recurrent confrontation of eye with stone.

(1)
"Severity"
Part IV is a short section of three poems: "Severity", "Tonight's News" and "Calm". "Severity" echoes its parent poem, Derek Walcott's "The Brother".[72] It proposes preposterous punishments, Judge Dreadword-style, for a bizarre list of annoyances. Insincerity, disguised as love or admiration must be blinded, shot and crucified. Women's proclaimed love, particularly that of a wife, is one form of severely punishable hypocrisy. The fawning approval of literary critics when stripped of its camouflage is revealed to be merciless, cowardly sniping done from smug, safe academic distance.

> Every poet is a wanted man; stay from your cave on the hill
> and pick them off like the flies they are. Life is a
> mean quick draw, it will kill you at high noon
> and leave you for the circling crows

288

Suspicious of all persons and things, the sequestered narrator sinks ever more deeply into paranoia.

Stab

All those who say they come to help.

The worst of such hypocrites is the wife:

> That ringed helping hand offering a warm bed and hot night-cap must be slashed.

We have circled back to the domestic tedium of "Housework", viewed now through the cold eye of a consciousness that is more driven, manic and violent. Staring past this hyperbole of violent punishments, one sees a beleaguered protagonist at the end of his tether and unable to cope with the noises of his environment ranging from the smug mouthings of a television commentator, the scream of a child and incessant steelband music, to the neighbours' "deranged stereo" and their loud constant quarrelling.

All of these maddening sounds combine to release a rage that, uncontained by his grotesque laughter, issues through crevices of his subterranean self. In such minds, there is always a latent possibility of the gruesome rhetoric and wordplay of violence becoming reality. Yet as one leaves the poem the impression is that the poet retains a control that his protagonist or voice in the poem has lost. Noise and the cycle of domestic routine frustrate his effort to "ride into the forest of paper/alone", that is, to complete his dissertation of over six hundred pages, or to fulfil the Herculean objectives he has set himself in his effort to live the life of a writer, poet and academic.

The image of the poet riding into a forest of paper "in the *dead* of night" after having magically "short-circuited" the neighbours' noisy stereo and "electrocuted" all ensuing shadows that hinder the fulfilment of his burdensome mission, is grimly comical, mock-heroic and typical of Questel's self-reducing irony. It deflates his illusions of being Clint Eastwood, Lee van Cleef or even Gregory Peck delivering bullet-ridden cowboy justice to wretched one-hoss frontier towns. It mocks gently at Yeats's and Harris's cold-eyed horseman riding by through death's portal into the challenge of some unknown other dimension. It replaces the psychopath of domestic violence, that gremlin judge and executioner who resides in the darkness of his subconscious, with the homelier, more familiar and helpless figure of the graduate student trying to find silence and space to think in a noise-polluted environment.

(2)
"Tonight's News"
"Tonight's News" extends the "dead of night" metaphor of the preceding poem, and is a metaphor of the subconscious, the dark night of the soul, the night journey. This final journey into night reveals not dread, but stillness, nothing, no one, darkness. This is a silence far beyond that which the graduate student, stoned by external noises, sought. Travelling inward the narrator of "Tonight" hits "rock bottom" in his cave of being.

> The light is dim. The presenter is not
> In focus. In fact there are no people there.
> Nothing. It is now dark in this cave.

Yet in the cave's gloom he somehow perceives Timehri, Harrisian rock drawings, markings on the wall.[73] Such language, the calligraphy of other peoples' ancestors, is indecipherable to the dreamer. What is one to make of a time, people and civilization, long erased, but whose signs are still dimly visible in one's cave of dreams?

The poem does not say. The traveller arises abruptly from his dream of the beginning of time to predict the future. It isn't one of renewal but of death, whose omens, now that he has ascended out of his cave of silence, are both clearly visible and audible. Death's visible road-sign is something "beneath this sheet" at which the reader is invited to "Stare". Death's audible sign is the neighbour's short-circuited stereo coming to life again with the sudden scream of a gospel singer. Is this scream a sign of hope, affirmation or hysteria? Significantly, she screams "from the dust jacket of her disc". She too is caught up in spinning circles and enclosed in her envelope or jacket of dust – that is, the body; the flesh that is or will become, as Ash-Wednesday priests remind the penitent, ash, dust. The fact that her voice penetrates beyond his future does suggest that it is part of the eternal energy of life itself. As the rock drawings have made the past visible, so the recorded voice can be imagined to transcend time and death.

This epiphany brings little real hope to the poet, who recognizes that his future, like everyone else's, is to die, a fact that can be outscreamed, perhaps, but never outstared.

"Calm"

"Calm" follows directly from "Tonight's News". Its first line – "A calm is settling on him again; he is dead-/ beat" tells us that though Questel, objectified and distanced from himself by the third-person "he", isn't dead, he is exhausted after inner turmoil, with the weariness unto death. "Calm" speaks not so much of an Aristotelian catharsis after experiencing a surfeit of pity and terror, as of exhaustion in the aftermath of "a temporary breakdown", a fever, a too hard "staring at pools of silence".

> He stops staring at pools of silence.
> It was not the final night;
> just a breaker tripping off –
> a temporary breakdown;

The electricity images with which *Hard Stares* is replete (the light bulb and connecting cable in "Downstairs"; the references to electrocution and short-circuiting in "Severity", or the electric chair that, in his dream of retribution, the narrator of "Footfalls" reserves for his murderous dictator) are now applied by Questel to his own private situation of breakdown and blackout, so graphically portrayed earlier in "Coconut". Wryly, wanly he diagnoses his problem as "just a breaker tripping off". Employing for the last time imagery derived from music, he describes his attack as having been "*minor* and low-keyed." One notes the association of the minor mode with sadness. Questel does not dwell on this note of sadness, but as his morning of convalescence progresses, re-enters the world of Sartre's Roquentin where normally inert objects reveal a malevolent potential and agency. In "Calm", the convalescent needs to reconcile himself to a menace of things animated by the same electricity that has restored light and life to his darkened mind.

The circle is complete. In the title poem, "Hard Stares", the toast, perforated with holes, is an image of experience, fixed taut by searing vision, and of the mind, dried brittle and on the verge of collapse. Here we have the comic reduction of the assassination motif. The poet who no longer has to dodge snipers' attacks from the "cave on the hill", knows that he still has to keep his eyes on that hostile electric toaster. Far from being a knight-errant riding past demons into the forest of the night as he jestingly imagined himself to be in "Severity", Questel's protagonist, on awakening, re-enters the Absurd universe of visible, malevolent things, where he resumes his mission of bridging with laughter the ever-narrowing divide between insanity and sanity.

Gordon Rohlehr
23 August 2015 – 07 September 2015

Endnotes

1. Kamau Brathwaite, "Negus", *The Arrivants* (London: Oxford University Press, 1973), 222-224.
2. Victor Questel, *De Doctor – He Dead* 1970. Staged 1974, Port of Spain.
3. Roger McTair, "Corners Without Answers," in Clifford Sealey, (ed). *Voices,* I, No 1 (August, 1964).
4. Derek Walcott, "Codicil", in *The Castaway and other Poems* (London: Jonathan Cape, 1965), 61.
5. Victor Questel, "Walcott's Hack's Hired Prose", Bibliography of Walcott's articles on Architecture, Painting and Sculpture", *Kairi* '78, 64-67.
6. Kamau Brathwaite, "Negus", *The Arrivants* (London: Oxford University Press, 1973), 224.
7. Ibid.
8. Victor Questel, "Lines" for Robert Lee, *Collected Poems, 84-86.*
9. Victor Questel, *Score: Poems by Victor D. Questel and Anson Gonzalez* (Port of Spain: 1972).
10. Derek Walcott, "Prelude", *In a Green Night: Poems 1948-1960*, (London: Jonathan Cape, 1962, 11.
11. V.S. Naipaul, *Guerillas* (London: Andre Deutsch, 1975).
12. Derek Walcott, "The Castaway", *The Castaway and other Poems,* (London: Jonathan Cape, 1965).
13. E.M. Roach, "Love Overgrows a Rock", *The Flowering Rock: Collected Poems 1938-1974* (Leeds: Peepal Tree, 1991), 127. Poem originally published in 1957.
14. Kamau Brathwaite, "The Zoo", *BIM,* No 39, 1964.
15. Kamau Brathwaite, "Leopard", *The Arrivants* (London: OUP, 1973) 224.
16. Derek Walcott, "What the Twilight Says: an Overture", *Dream on Monkey Mountain and Other Plays* (New York: Farrar, Straus & Giroux, 1970).
17. Rene Gerard, *Things Hidden Since the Foundation of the World,* (Stanford: California, Stanford University Press, 1987).
18. T.S. Eliot, "The Hollow Men", *Collected Poems 1909-1935* (London: Faber & Faber Lit., 1958), 87-90.

19. Words cited from the National Anthem of Trinidad and Tobago.

20. Derek Walcott, "A Far Cry from Africa", *In a Green Night: Poems 1948-1960* (London: Jonathan Cape, 1962), 18; "Ruins of a Great House", ibid, 19-20.

21. Ibid, 25.

22. Victor Questel, "Linkages", *Score* (Port of Spain, 1972), 26.

23. Kamau Brathwaite, *The Arrivants* (London: OUP, 1973), 119.

24. Derek Walcott, "What the Twilight Says: an Overture", *Dream on Monkey Mountain and Other Plays* (New York, Farrar: Strauss & Giroux, 1970).

25. Derek Walcott, "Hic Jacet", *The Gulf and Other Poems* (London: Jonathan Cape, 1969), 70-71.

26. Winston Hackett, "Survival," *Tapia* V, No. 34 (Sunday August 24, 1975) and *Tapia,* No. 36 (Sunday September 7, 1975)

27. "Sea Blast" (18 July 1976).

28. Glen Campbell, "Gentle on My Mind", *Very Best of Glen Campbell.*

29. Cf Kamau Brathwaite, "The Golden Stool", *Masks*, *The Arrivants* (London: OUP, 1973), 146.

30. Derek Walcott, "Nights in the Garden of Port of Spain", *The Castaway and Other Poems* (London: Jonathan Cape, 1965), 43.

31. See Dante's *Inferno* or Virgil's *Aeneid* Bk. VI.

32. Wilson Harris, *The Far Journey of Oudin* (London: Faber & Faber, 1961).

33. Derek Walcott, "A Village Life", *The Castaway and Other Poems* (London: Jonathan Cape, 1965).

34. See George Lamming, *In the Castle of My Skin* and *Of Age and Innocence;* Derek Walcott, "Sea Crab"; Kamau Brathwaite, "Crab"; Faustin Charles, *Crab Track.*

35. Gordon Rohlehr, "My Strangled City", *My Strangled City and other Essays* (Port of Spain: Longman Trinidad Limited, 1992), 205-222.

36. J.D. Elder, *From Congo Drum to Steelband* (Port of Spain, 1969).

37. Kamau Brathwaite, *The Arrivants* (London: OUP, 1973), 263.

38. Derek Walcott, "The Sea is History", *The Star Apple Kingdom* (New York: Farrar, Straus & Giroux, 1977), 25.

39. Derek Walcott, "Mass Man", *The Gulf & Other Poems* (London: Jonathan Cape, 1969), 19; "Junta", ibid, 18.

40. Derek Walcott, *Ti Jean and His Brothers* in *Dream on Monkey Mountain and other Plays* (New York: Farrar Straus, Giroux, 1970).

41. Amos Tutuola, *The Palm Wine Drinkard* (New York: Grove Press Inc., 1953), 68.

42. Derek Walcott, "The Figure of Crusoe: On the Theme of Isolation in West Indian Writing", Typescript, UWI Library St Augustine, Trinidad and Tobago, 1965.

43. O. Mannoni, *Prospero and Caliban: The Psychology of Colonization* (New York: Praeger, 1964). First published Paris, Editions du Seuil, 1950); Frantz Fanon, *The Wretched of the Earth* (New York: Grove Press, 1963); Albert Memmi, *The*

Colonizer and the Colonized (Boston: Beacon Press, 1967).

44. Kamau Brathwaite, "4ᵗʰ Traveller", *Dream Stories* (Essex: Longman Group Ltd, 1994), 92.

45. Eric Williams, "Politics and Culture", *PNM Weekly*, Vol 2 No 52, Monday September 1, 1958.

46. Kamau Brathwaite, "Negus", *The Arrivants*, 1972, 224.

47. Ibid, 265.

48. Derek Walcott, "Pocomania", *In a Green Night: Poems 1948-1960* (London: Jonathan Cape, 1962), 35.

49. Max Romeo, "Macabee Version", 1970.

50. Derek Walcott, "In a Green Night" *In a Green Night: Poems 1948-1960*, 73.

51. Basil Mathews, *Crisis of the West Indian Family* (Port of Spain: UWI Extra-Mural Dept., 1952).

52. The Mighty Sparrow, "Gunslingers", 1959; Leveller, "How to Curb Delinquency", 1966.

53. Kamau Brathwaite, "The Making of the Drum", *Masks, The Arrivants*, 1973, 94.

54. I.e. the Muslimeen uprising of 1990, Trinidad and Tobago.

55. Kamau Brathwaite, "Jah", *The Arrivants*, 1973, 162-163.

56. Ibid, 185-188.

57. Kamau Brathwaite, "Ogun", *The Arrivants*, 243.

58. Ellsworth ("Shake") Keane, "Calypso Dancers" in *L'Oubli*, Barbados, 1950, 27-30.

59. E.g. Edgar Mittelholzer's *My Bones and My Flute* or Alejo Carpentier's *The Lost Steps.*

60. Kamau Brathwaite, "Fetish", *Third World Poems* (Harlow-Essex: Longman 1983), 3-4. First published in *Black+Blues*, 1976.

61. "Marian Questel Says Thanks", *The New Voices Newsletter,* Vol. III, No 1, 21ˢᵗ June, 1983.

62. See e.g. Sparrow's "Royal Jail", (1960).

63. Dylan Thomas, "Do not go gentle into that good night", *The Poems* (London: J.M. Dent, 1971), 207.

64. Prince Buster, "Judge Dread". See also, "The Appeal" and "Barrister Pardon" by the same singer.

65. Wilson Harris, *Palace of the Peacock* (London: Faber & Faber, 1960).

66. Derek Walcott, "Guyana", "The White Town", *The Gulf and Other Poems* (London: Jonathan Cape, 1969), 40.

67. Joseph Conrad, "Autocracy and War", *Notes on Life and Letters, Fortnightly Review*, July 1905.

68. Linden Forbes Burnham, *A Destiny to Mould: Selected Discourses by the Prime Minister of Guyana* (Georgetown: Longman Caribbean, 1970).

69. See e.g. Jimmy Ramsahoye, *A Mouldy Destiny: Visiting Guyana's Forbes Burnham* (Minerva Press, 1996).

70. Albert Camus, *The Myth of Sisyphus* (Paris: Seuil, 1942; London: Penguin, 1955)

71. In "Numb", Questel describes himself as "beer-scented, lucid, comical."

72. Derek Walcott, "The Brother", *Sea Grapes* (London: Jonathan Cape 1976), 23-24.

73. Wilson Harris, *The Sleepers of Roraima* (London: Faber and Faber, 1970).

ABOUT THE AUTHORS

Victor D. Questel was born in Gonzalez village in 1949. He attended Trinity College and the University of the West Indies at St Augustine. At UWI he was the first student in the Department of English to be awarded a Ph D for his thesis on the work of Derek Walcott. He earned a living as a teacher and reviewer. He died suddenly in April 1982. In addition to his three poetry collections, he published widely in journals and in anthologies such as *Now*, *Caribbean Rhythms*, *Melanthika* and *The Penguin Book of Caribbean Verse*.

Gordon Rohlehr is Emeritus Professor at the University of the West Indies at St Augustine. He is unquestionably one of the Caribbean's finest critics and thinkers. His territory covers both literature and popular culture, particularly Calypso. His publications include: *Pathfinder: Black Awakening in "The Arrivants" of Edward Kamau Brathwaite* (Tunapuna: College Press, 1981); *Cultural Resistance and the Guyana State* (Casa de las Américas, 1984); *Calypso and Society in Pre-Independence Trinidad* (Port of Spain, 1989); *My Strangled City and Other Essays* (Longman Trinidad, 1992); *The Shape of That Hurt and Other Essays* (Longman Trinidad, 1992); *A Scuffling of Islands: Essays on Calypso* (Lexicon Trinidad Ltd, 2004); *Transgression, Transition, Transformation: Essays in Caribbean Culture* (Lexicon, 2007); and *Ancestories: Readings of Kamau Brathwaite's "Ancestors"* (Trinidad: Lexicon, 2010) and *My Whole Life is Calypso: Essays on Sparrow* (Trinidad: The Blue Edition, 2015).

RELATED TITLES

Anson Gonzalez
Artefacts of Presence: Collected Poems 1964-2000
ISBN: 9781845230357; pp. 242; pub. 2010; price £10.99

Those who have followed Anson Gonzalez's career will imagine they know his evolution from the engaged poet of the political turbulence of late 1960s, early 70's Trinidad revealed in *Score*, to the confessional poet who adopted the persona of a Caribbean Don Juan in *The Love-song of Boysie B.*, to the contemplative poet of spiritual exploration in *Moksha: Poems of Light and Sound* and *Merry-go-round and Other Poems*. In this new *Collected Poems*, along with a number of important new poems, Anson Gonzalez carefully disrupts such expectations by an arrangement that mixes poems from across the decades.

What this rearrangement reveals are consistencies of concern and approach, whatever the period. There is a compunction to truth-telling, however uncomfortable; there is a constant state of tension between the desire for involvement in the world (with the adoption of a prophetic voice to excoriate all that is unsatisfactory in it), and an attentiveness to the unbidden inner voices that speak of separateness and alienation; there is also an alertness to moments of unlooked for joy (and anguish) most often found in family and fatherhood. Above all, the poems speak of the impossibility of writing poems that do justice to the promptings that inspire them. In the process, Anson Gonzalez reveals himself as an everyman, an intensely Trinidadian man and a writer dedicated to the demands of art with his finger on the pulse of both the state of the nation and the state of the inner man.

Anson Gonzalez was a Trinidadian poet, critic, publisher and encourager of countless writing careers. He was Victor Questel's publisher and the founder and sustainer of *The New Voices* journal for many years. He died in 2015

Anson Gonzalez
Crossroads of Dream
ISBN: 9781900715898; pp. 72; pub. 2005; price £7.99

Anson Gonzalez's prose poems criss-cross the crossroads between dream and conscious awareness. They set the reader on a surreal adventure into the mental journeys of a persona for whom the inner and outer worlds are a seamless universe. There is no order to the presentation of the prose poems; they take their own twists and turns. The poems are lyrical, tell stories and explore a lifetime of reflective concern with life's conundrums: love, ageing, finding an inner purpose, being Trinidadian – and sometimes feeling out of step with the temper of the times. These poems are the work of one who hears a different drummer and their tone is sometimes sardonic, and even cynical – though always with a wry, self-deprecating humour. Above all, the twinkle in the tone suggests a healthy appreciation for humour of fickle fate or capricious gods. While there is ultimately no didactic purpose – the mind leads and the poet follows – these globules of consciousness in action both illuminate and delight.

These and over 350 Caribbean and Black British titles are available on line from peepaltreepress.com and by mail order from Peepal Tree Press, 17 Kings Avenue, Leeds LS6 1QS, or by phone +44 113 245 1703.